INTRODUCTORY PSYCHOLOGY

This series of titles is aimed at psychology students in sixth forms and further education colleges and at those wishing to obtain an overview of psychology. The books are easy to use, with comprehensive notes written in coherent language; clear flagging of key concepts; relevant and interesting illustrations; well-defined objectives and further reading sections to each chapter, and self-assessment questions at regular intervals throughout the text.

Published

INDIVIDUAL DIFFERENCES
Ann Birch and Sheila Hayward

DEVELOPMENTAL PSYCHOLOGY
Ann Birch and Tony Malim

BIOPSYCHOLOGY
Sheila Hayward

COGNITIVE PROCESSES
Tony Malim

COMPARATIVE PSYCHOLOGY
Tony Malim, Ann Birch and Sheila Hayward

RESEARCH METHODS AND STATISTICS
Tony Malim and Ann Birch

SOCIAL PSYCHOLOGY
Tony Malim and Ann Birch

PERSPECTIVES IN PSYCHOLOGY
Tony Malim, Ann Birch and Alison Wadeley

Series Standing Order

If you would like to receive future titles in this series as they are published, you can make use of our standing order facility. To place a standing order please contact your bookseller or, in case of difficulty, write to us at the address below with your name and address and the name of the series. Please state with which title you wish to begin your standing order. (If you live outside the United Kingdom we may not have the rights for your area, in which case we will forward your order to the publisher concerned.)

Customer Services Department, Macmillan Distribution Ltd
Houndmills, Basingstoke, Hampshire RG21 6XS, England

RESEARCH METHODS AND STATISTICS

Tony Malim and Ann Birch

MACMILLAN

First published 1997 by
MACMILLAN PRESS LTD
Houndmills, Basingstoke, Hampshire RG21 6XS
and London
Companies and representatives
throughout the world

ISBN 0–333–64439–5

A catalogue record for this book is available
from the British Library.

10   9   8   7   6   5   4   3   2   1
06 05 04 03 02 01 00 99 98 97

Editing and origination by
Aardvark Editorial, Mendham, Suffolk

Printed in Hong Kong

Cartoons by Sally Artz

Contents

List of Figures

Preface

Research Methods and Statistics is the final volume in the Introductory Psychology series, and its aims are similar to those of the other volumes in the series. Chapters 1 and 2 provide an introduction and an overview of some of the methods used in psychological research, highlighting the advantages and limitations of each. From Chapter 3 onwards, it becomes very much a workbook. Chapter 3 deals with the use of statistics in psychology to describe and to make inferences about data obtained through observations, and Chapter 4 is devoted to statistical testing. In Chapter 5, attention is paid to the way in which the results of research are interpreted and presented. Finally, in Chapter 6, several possible projects are outlined. Appendices include some very basic mathematical rules for those who are less familiar with the use of figures, guidance in making some do-it-yourself equipment which the authors have found useful, and some statistical tables for use in conjunction with the statistical procedures in Chapter 4.

The intention is that the book will provide practical help with the course work element of 'A' and 'AS' level syllabuses and the Research Methods modules. As in the other books in the series, each chapter begins with some objectives to be met, and at the end of each section there are self-assessment questions to help independent students test their understanding of the section. Readers are advised to work carefully through the text one section at a time before considering the self-assessment questions at the end of it. After further reading or study, the questions may be re-examined.

The book focuses primarily upon GCE 'A' and 'AS' levels and GCSE. However, it should prove useful to any one encountering psychology for the first time or indeed any students who need to use research methods and statistics. This might include perhaps biologists and students in other related disciplines. Students on university courses may find the contents valuable, as may those on BTEC/GNVQ courses, nurses, midwives and teachers. The authors hope that you will find the book both useful and enjoyable.

Tony Malim
Ann Birch

Acknowledgements

Permission has been granted in relation to the following:

Tables A, B, C, D, E, F and J are reproduced from J. Beer (1982) *Experiments in Psychology* published by Weidenfeld and Nicolson

Table I is reproduced from F. Clegg (1982) *Simple Statistics* published by Cambridge University Press

Tables G and H are reproduced from J.G. Snodgrass (1978) *The Numbers Game: Statistics for Psychology* published by Oxford University Press

The authors would like once again to thank Sally Artz for the cartoons which appear at the beginning of each chapter.

Personally, I'd be happy with a one-tailed hypothesis !

Introduction $\mathbf{1}$

INTRODUCTION

At the end of this chapter you should be able to:

1. identify and define some of the concepts in statistics and experimental design; and
2. list the ethical considerations which need to be borne in mind when conducting psychological research.

SECTION I   INTRODUCING SOME CONCEPTS AND TERMS USED IN STATISTICS AND RESEARCH

As you work through this book, you will be meeting a whole range of ideas which will be strange to you and which sometimes use words in a sense which is not the ordinary one. For this reason, we shall start by highlighting a number of ideas which you will meet later to ensure that you become familiar with them from the outset.

Populations and samples

Statisticians use the term **population** not to indicate a collection of people living in a particular place (as we might refer to the population of Great Britain), but to the group from which a sample is drawn. They may not, indeed, be people at all. They may be fish or even nuts and bolts! A manufacturer might be producing a certain kind of nut. This particular sort of nut would then be the 'population' from which the manufacturer might draw a sample every so often to test for strength or for some other property. A population need not actually exist at all. It might consist of numbers. The definition of population used by statisticians is as follows:

> any group of numbers, finite or infinite, which refer to real or hypothetical events. (Clegg, 1982, p 51)

Any numbers which have a common characteristic are included in this. It could be polar bears kept in zoos in Russia or 11+ test results from a group of children in Aberdeen, that is, just a set of scores. Populations can be small or large, the stars in the universe or National Lottery jackpot winners for example.

Representative samples

Samples are useful in that they allow researchers to examine the characteristics of the population with which they are concerned without going to the lengths of a detailed examination of the whole of it. Part of a statistician's skill lies in finding samples that are representative of the population from which they are drawn, so that generalisations can be made to the rest of it. It would not be much use just testing the last 30 nuts produced on a Friday afternoon. 'Representative' implies that the sample accurately reflects the composition of the population from which it is drawn; it has the same characteristics (apart from its size) in the same proportion. If the sample is truly representative, you will be able to generalise your results to the whole population.

There are various ways in which this **representative sample** can be approached. Although it is hard, if not impossible, to *guarantee* a representative sample, you can reduce the chance of bias:

- It may be a **random sample**. This term has a very particular meaning to statisticians. Every member of the population needs to have an equal chance of being represented.

Supposing that you were concerned with a population of schoolchildren (perhaps to test their retention of what they had been taught); every child in the population needs to have an equal chance of being picked for testing. Returning to the problems inherent in obtaining a random sample of people for psychological research, you first need accurately to define the population. Suppose, for example, you choose to define your population as 'Londoners'; do you mean all those who *live* in London, all those who were born there, or perhaps all those who make their living there? In any of these cases, you would need to devise a way in which you could select a sample in which each and every member of the population had an equal chance of being selected. It could be very difficult. If you chose to use a telephone directory, you run up against the problem that not everyone has a telephone, so that you would get a random sample of London telephone subscribers rather than of 'Londoners'. You might think of using the electoral role, but then you would exclude all those under the age of 18, all foreigners and anyone who for some reason or another had not registered to vote. Your random sample would then be from a population of electors in London, not Londoners.

The answer lies in the careful definition of the population. If you define your population as children attending St George's School (wherever that might be) it is a comparatively simple matter to obtain a list of all those children, write each name on a slip of paper, put the slips into a tombola and draw out however many you needed – bingo! a random sample. Alternatively, you could assign a number to each child on the list and then consult a table of random numbers (there is one included in Appendix III of this book). It is a simple matter to obtain your sample. Just open the table, close your eyes and use a pin to light upon a number. That number represents an individual member of your population. You can go on doing this until you have enough for your sample. Suppose, however, that you were trying to compare the performance in some respect of girls and boys in St George's School. Then you have in effect two populations, one of girls and one of boys, and you would have to go about producing your two samples from the two populations in the same way as has been described. You could, of course, get a computer to generate random numbers, in much the same way as ERNIE does for Premium Bond draws, or use the kind of tombola used in the draws for the National Lottery. A random sample has a good chance of being representative of the population from which it is drawn so that you can generalise your findings from observations you have made of the sample and reasonably suggest that they might be true of the whole population. At the very least, the method by which your sample is chosen is free from bias.

So, here is the procedure:

1. Define the population.
2. Establish a list of all the members of that population.
3. Assign a number to each member.
4. Generate random numbers up to the size of the sample(s) you require.
5. Apply the numbers to your list, and you have your sample(s).

■ **Exercise 1.1**

You want to compare the lifestyles of pensioners in Brighton and Biarritz.

1. What are your populations?
2. How could you go about drawing up random samples from these populations?

● An alternative way to obtain a representative sample is to use a **quota sample**. This is frequently used in surveys. You select characteristics which you consider important as far as your study is concerned. You then systematically choose individuals who possess these characteristics in the same proportions as the population as a whole. You might decide that the important characteristics you needed to consider are sex, age and socioeconomic status. Your sample would need to include individuals who display these characteristics in equal proportion to those evident in the whole population. For instance, you reckon that the proportion of males and females in the population is 50:50, so that your sample would need to include 50 per cent males and 50 per cent females. As far as age is concerned, you could establish broad categories, say, under 20, 20–50 and over 50. A preliminary survey might have shown that the proportions of the three age groups in the population were 20 per cent, 40 per cent and 60 per cent respectively. Your sample would include people from each of these age ranges in the same proportions. As far as socioeconomic status is concerned, you could operate similarly, using a scale of social classes, based upon occupation. Again, a preliminary survey would show you what the proportions of each class were in the population. Your sample would be made up in the same proportions. In this way, you can claim the sample to be representative, at least as far as the selected characteristics are concerned.

- Another sampling method is known as **stratified sampling**. This requires a fairly detailed knowledge of the population you are studying, to establish strata or subgroups within the population. Within a school, these subgroups might include year groups, males and females, or perhaps sets or streams. From these population subgroups, you can proceed systematically to draw random samples of the kind described above in the same proportions as in the parent population.

- Yet another way of obtaining a representative sample is **cluster sampling**. This is based on the existence of natural groups. It might be families, or houses on an estate, or children in a class. The natural groups are numbered, and a random sample is drawn from these numbers. It might work like this. Within all the primary schools in a particular county, the reception classes are identified and numbered. Suppose there are 45 in all, and you wanted a sample of 300 individual children. Assuming roughly 30 children to a class, you would need to draw 10 classes randomly from your 45. Once this was done, you might identify and study in detail particular subgroups, perhaps children under five on entry compared with those over five. This provides you with a representative sample of a large population in a fairly economical way. Unfortunately, there are also risks involved.

If one of the clusters chosen happens to be unrepresentative in some way, you have introduced some **systematic error**.

● The aim is always to obtain a sample or samples which are fully representative of the population from which they are drawn. However, this may not always be possible. An **opportunity sample** is sometimes used, which simply employs those individuals who are available at the time the study is done. It has to be remembered, though, that opportunity samples may not be representative. There must be caution in the way in which such studies are interpreted. Generalisation from such results can be risky. Project 5 in Chapter 6 employs an opportunity sample of people who happen to be passing a particular set of traffic lights at a particular time. Opportunity samples are commonly used by students as they are the easiest to obtain and they do have value in providing a preliminary indication of results, but you need to be aware of their limitations regarding generalisation.

Errors – systematic and random

Being fallible humans living in a less than perfect world, there is always the chance that error may occur. One of the purposes of the use of statistics is to allow for this **random error**. You are never going to be able to eliminate it. **Systematic error**, on the other hand, needs to be guarded against and avoided at all costs. This happens where poor research design has allowed a bias to occur which consistently favours one condition in an investigation rather than another. It could be due to sampling error (as above) or perhaps to **order effects** or to some other foreseeable and preventable source of bias. Chapter 2, Section II will address some of the ways in which sources of systematic error may be brought under control.

Theories and hypotheses

Someone who is engaged in research will from time to time formulate a **theory**. This amounts to a statement of what the findings of the research carried out thus far seem to show. It is usually fairly general in its nature and not in a form in which it can readily be tested. Essentially, it amounts to an overall picture of where the research seems to be leading. Let us take an example.

In researching the nature of memory, Peterson and Peterson (1959) came to the conclusion that when something was memorised, there was what they termed a **memory trace** within the brain. This trace gradually decayed over time, and this led to forgetting. They had found that after short intervals of time (for example three to six seconds), recall was generally quite good, but after about 18 seconds much of what had been encountered had been forgotten. They put forward their **trace–decay theory**, that is, their explanation of what they had found. Later alternative explanations included an **interference** theory of forgetting, which suggested that other material was interfering with what had to be recalled. Either of these theories represented an explanation of what had been found thus far and provided a basis for further research to test which theory best explained what had been observed.

A theory is not, as it stands, testable, as it is too imprecise. In order to test it, it needs to be transposed into the form of a **hypothesis**, that is, a prediction of outcomes in specific circumstances. To do this, each bit of the theory needs to be carefully defined and **operationalised**. That is to say, it needs to be put into a form which can be tested by experiment, observation or some other form of investigation, such as a correlational study or a survey.

Supposing we start with a theory that time during which you are doing nothing is perceived as being longer than time which is fully occupied. That in its present form is not testable, but it can be converted into a hypothesis by operationalising it. You start by identifying precisely what is meant by 'doing nothing'. It might be sitting at an empty table with both mind and body entirely unoccupied. In contrast to this, 'occupied time' might be defined as time spent with a pair of compasses and a sheet of paper, constructing as many designs as possible. It does not much matter what the occupation is as long as it is defined and clearly something which can be put into practice. It will probably not embrace all the theory. In this instance, 'occupation' might be defined as mental occupation or physical occupation, so that the theory might be operationalised in two ways. Then the researcher will need to tackle the idea of 'perception of time'. This might involve an estimate of time spent. The hypothesis might then be stated as a prediction in some such terms as these:

People who sit at an empty table with both mind and body entirely unoccupied will overestimate the time that elapses; while if they are actively engaged creating designs on a sheet of paper with a pair of compasses, they will underestimate it.

■ **Exercise 1.2**

Take the following theory and operationalise it as a hypothesis. 'Watching violence on TV results in an increase in aggression.' Define your terms carefully and make a prediction based upon the theoretical idea above. (The answer is after the self-assessment questions.)

Null and alternative hypotheses

A **null hypothesis (H_0)** amounts to a prediction that any difference or similarity found could have been the result of chance variability (perhaps errors in measurement, sampling, the variability of human beings or some other random error), rather than to the real phenomenon you are trying to observe and measure. The sample of the population you happen to have taken may not be representative of the population. Retention of the null hypothesis implies that your data indicate that the samples you are looking at are just different samples from the same population, and that the variations you are observing are the result of your sampling and not of any difference between the populations: you just happen to have observed chance variations within the same population. The more observations you take, the less the effect of chance is going to be. For instance, in the example quoted above, retention of the null hypothesis would mean that what you have been observing were just samples from a single population of people, rather than from two populations, one of unoccupied people, the other of occupied people. In other words, your results could have occurred by chance alone.

The **alternative hypothesis** (H_α) accepts that your observations have convinced you that you are observing a real phenomenon and that differences or similarities are not just due to chance. You are, in effect, not looking at two samples from one population but samples from two different populations. There are three ways of reaching this conclusion:

1. Go on making a sufficient number of observations and measurements to convince yourself that there is no reasonable doubt that what you were observing was a real phenomenon.
2. Maybe the differences you have observed are large enough to convince you of this straight away, but this is not usually the case.
3. You may not have the resources to make sufficient observations and measurements to ensure that chance can be ruled out. Therefore, you work out the statistical probability that the observations you are making are due to chance, that you are in fact just looking at two samples of one population. Let us take an example. Suppose you are theoretically interested in the notion that only children do better in school than those who come from large families. You find samples of each of the populations in question, ensuring that they are representative. You then test the school performance of each sample. The null hypothesis assumes that what you are looking at are just two samples from a single population of children. The alternative hypothesis is that this is not the case. There are indeed two samples from two different populations, one of only children with better school performance, the other of children from large families who have inferior school performance. What a statistical test of inference will enable you to do is to assess the probability that the predictions of the null hypothesis are true: that there is no difference or similarity between the samples except that which is due to chance. It is up to you then to retain or to reject the null hypothesis on the basis of that probability.

Chapter 3 deals with the use of statistics, first to describe accurately what is being observed and then to make inferences as to what would be the likely outcome if you went on making similar observations a very much larger number of times.

One tail or two tails?

A hypothesis may be said to be **one-tailed** or **two-tailed**. This has nothing to do with physiology. A one-tailed hypothesis is directional; a two-tailed hypothesis is non-directional. For example, if you predict that drinking coffee will improve your learning scores that is directional. Whereas if you predict just that there will be an effect on learning scores from drinking coffee that is non-directional.

Significance and confidence levels

The term **significance** is used in connection with the acceptance of the alternative hypothesis. If you have become convinced of the reality of the phenomenon you are observing by any of the three means described above, then the difference (or the similarity in the case of correlational studies) is described as being **significant**. You have confidence that what you are observing is not just a chance occurrence. There has to be a point at which you can have this confidence. If, as is most likely, you have worked out the statistical probability of what you are observing occurring by chance, you need to establish a **confidence level**. Your statistical test (these are described in detail in Chapters 3 and 4) will show the probability (p) that your results could have been due to chance as a percentage (most often, equal to or less than 5 per cent or equal to or less than 1 per cent probability). This is also expressed as a decimal fraction ($p \leq 0.05$ or $p \leq 0.01$). Which confidence level you choose is up to you, the researcher, but there are implications.

Type I and type II errors

Whichever choice you make, there is a risk of error. These can be what are termed **type I** or **type II** errors.

A type I error occurs when you reject the null hypothesis and accept the alternative hypothesis (H_α) when there is no real difference (or similarity).

A type II error is the converse of this. You have retained the null hypothesis and concluded that there is no real effect observed, when in fact there is a real difference (or similarity).

Type I and type II errors are fully discussed in Chapter 3.

Self-assessment questions

1. Briefly define the terms 'null hypothesis' and 'type II error'.
2. Define a 'population' and a 'sample'. Describe two ways of obtaining a representative sample.
3. List two different experimental designs. Identify the advantages and disadvantages of each.

■ ■ ANSWER TO EXERCISE 1.2

Children (aged 10–12) who watch violent programmes on TV for two hours every evening will display a greater number of aggressive incidents of behaviour than children who watch a similar amount of non-violent TV.

SECTION II   ETHICAL QUESTIONS IN RELATION TO RESEARCH

It is important that anyone who engages in psychological research is aware that, whenever research is carried out, there may be ethical implications. This section aims to outline some of the considerations which need to be borne in mind in order to ensure that any research carried out is in accordance with ethical guidelines. The authors have made reference to articles which appeared in *Psychology Teaching* (Davies, 1992; Davies *et al.*, 1992), for which we are indebted. While what is contained in this section refers primarily to those carrying out research studies as part of an 'A' level course, it applies equally to anyone engaged in similar work.

Davies and his colleagues have outlined what should be considered under four main headings:

1. **Competence**
2. **Consent**
3. **Confidentiality**
4. **Conduct.**

Competence

This is relevant to students working at an introductory level, whose enthusiasm may well outstrip their competence. For example, the use of psychometric tests is subject to guidelines laid down by the British Psychological Society (BPS), who have clearly set out the training requirements for the use of particular tests. It is unethical for anyone who has not received the requisite training to use these tests. If there is any doubt whether you are competent to carry through any aspect of the study you have embarked upon, you must seek advice – in the first instance from your teacher, lecturer or supervisor.

Consent

Informed consent is central to the use of any human participants in a psychological study. In many instances, informed consent will not be difficult to obtain. Fellow students will be keen enough to take part. In all cases, it is up to you to ensure that participants are fully informed of the aims of the study and so fully understand what they are agreeing to. There are a number of related issues, outlined below.

Deception

It is unethical to deceive participants or to withhold information about the purposes of the study. There may be occasions when you need to carry out a 'blind' study; it may not be possible to control 'demand characteristics' in any other way. In such circumstances, it should be made quite clear to the participants what you are doing and why, and they should be fully debriefed when the study is over. If you think that participants are likely to be distressed or upset by what you tell them afterwards, you ought not to carry out the study.

Participants' right to withdraw

If at any point participants want to withdraw, they should be free to do so. They should be given to understand at the outset that this is the case. No pressure should be exerted on them to continue, no matter how inconvenient it may be for you. Furthermore, once the investigation has been completed, participants have the right to withdraw their permission to use the data obtained.

Consent for children to participate

The informed consent of children does present some problems. Even if they can reasonably be expected to understand fully what it is they are agreeing to, you need to make sure you have the consent of a parent or guardian, or, failing this, of a responsible adult who has charge of the child at the time. You may sometimes want to conduct research within a school or a playgroup. Clearly, head teachers or the playgroup leaders need to give their informed consent, but you may also need to obtain parental consent if the head teacher thinks you should.

You should, of course, also ask the children themselves whether they wish to take part.

Observation of behaviour in public

While it is not strictly necessary to obtain the consent of those whose behaviour you observe in public places, there are precautions to observe. You need to avoid doing anything which may concern, alarm or outrage members of the public. I recall a study of bystander apathy which resulted in students being brought before the local superintendent of police and rebuked: a bystander had informed them that a mugging was taking place. It is as well to inform and to seek the consent of the relevant authorities.

Confidentiality

The privacy of participants should be respected. There are a number of precautions to be taken:

1. Reports on studies completed should not include anything which may allow participants to be identified.
2. Numbers or initials should be used rather than names.
3. Let participants know if you intend to discuss the study with anyone else, including your teacher, lecturer or supervisor.

4. Make sure that your records cannot fall into the hands of any unauthorised individual.
5. Let your participants know beforehand what you will do with the report on the study and who will see it. As you conduct your study, it is possible that you may receive information that is sensitive – about criminal behaviour, for example. In such cases, you have to be bound by the law of the land, and concealing information about criminal behaviour is in itself a crime. This poses a dilemma for researchers, and it is preferable for investigations to be so designed that they do not obtain such information.

Conduct

The way in which your study is conducted is also important. Davies and his colleagues have listed some important things to avoid:

● insulting, offending or angering participants;
● making participants believe they have upset or harmed someone else;
● breaking the law or encouraging others to do so;
● contravening the Data Protection Act (that is to say, storing personal data on computer without proper registration, or using data for a purpose for which it has not been registered; for example, students might be tempted to use school records. These are unlikely to have been registered for this purpose under the Data Protection Act);
● copying tests or materials illegally;
● inventing data; and
● copying other people's work and claiming it as your own.

In general it is important that you do nothing which may cause insult or embarrassment, or which may be dangerous, painful or illegal.

Studies involving animals

In general, it is probably better to avoid the study of nonhuman species, and any form of experimentation is anyway illegal without a Home Office licence. There are fewer problems associated with field observation of animals, but even in this case great care needs to be taken to avoid disturbance or anything that may result in distress.

Ethical questions relating to psychological research are considered fully in Chapter 6 of *Perspectives in Psychology* (Malim *et al.*, 1992), and the British Psychological Society has produced a set of ethical guidelines (BPS 1990). It is essential that anyone thinking of engaging in psychological research should study these carefully.

Self-assessment questions

1. List some ethical considerations of which students doing psychological research need to be aware.
2. What is meant by 'informed consent?' What difficulties may occur in obtaining consent, particularly that of children?
3. List some steps that should be taken to ensure the confidentiality of psychological studies.
4. Make a list of things that a researcher should at all costs avoid.

FURTHER READING

Davies, G., Haworth, G. and Hirschler, S. (1992) Ethical issues in psychological research, in *Psychology Teaching* New Series (No.1), 4–10

British Psychological Society (1990) *Ethical Principles for Conducting Research with Human Participants* (Leicester: The British Psychological Society)

If none of us knows what the experiment is all about, why are we doing it?

Research Methods 2

At the end of this chapter you will be able to:

1. list and describe some examples of methods commonly used in psychological research. These may include experiment, observation, survey and case study methods;
2. make an evaluation of the strengths and weaknesses of each method; and
3. identify the kinds of research problems for which it is appropriate to use each method.

SECTION I   EXPERIMENT

The term **experiment** is frequently used (wrongly) to refer to a wide range of research procedures. It is necessary at an early stage to make quite clear what the term relates to. In an experiment, the researcher deliberately isolates and and manipulates one variable (referred to as the **independent variable [IV]**) at a time in order to observe and measure the effect of this manipulation upon another variable (the **dependent variable [DV]**). There will almost inevitably be other factors which will interfere to cloud the link between IV and DV. These are referred to as **extraneous** or **confounding variables**. An example will make this clearer.

A researcher has noticed that many young people have music on when they are studying. The suggestion has been made that this might have an adverse effect on their learning. In order to set up an experiment to examine the effect of background music upon learning, some definitions need to be established. The IV (the presence or absence of music) needs to be carefully defined. It might be pop, classical or jazz music, for example. It might be loud or quiet. It might be delivered through headphones or by means of a speaker. Similarly, the DV (learning) needs careful definition. It might be the recall of key facts from what has been studied. Extraneous variables needing to be controlled might include:

● the effect of wearing headphones;
● how used the participants are to listening to music;
● the physical conditions of the experiment: lighting, heating, seating, and so on; and
● the age, sex and academic ability of the participants.

Experimentation may be conducted in different settings – in a laboratory, in the field or in a natural setting. To illustrate this, here are some examples:

Laboratory experiment

Hess (1959) conducted a series of experiments to study the phenomenon of imprinting in ducklings. This is the natural process whereby the young of certain species form an attachment to the first moving thing they see after hatching. This has a clear survival value in the wild. The ducklings were hatched in an incubator in the laboratory. The first moving thing the newly hatched ducklings saw was a plastic model of a mallard duck on a revolving turntable. In the relatively controlled conditions of the laboratory, this was comparatively easy to bring about. The animals became imprinted on the plastic model and followed it on its travels round the turntable. In this way, Hess was able to identify the timing of the critical periods after hatching, when exposure to the model was most likely to result in imprinting. He could accurately control the time when the ducklings were exposed to their 'mother' and observe imprinting as it occurred. In this experiment, the independent variable was the time between hatching and exposure to the plastic model; the dependent variable was the imprinting of the ducklings on their 'mother'. Extraneous variables which needed to be controlled included any other moving thing which might come within sight of the ducklings, the speed of the revolving turntable and the lighting in the laboratory.

Field experiment

Tinbergen and Perdeck (1950) conducted a field experiment in the same area of study, animal behaviour. While Hess's study was conducted in a laboratory, Tinbergen and Perdeck's study was in the 'real world'. Herring gulls nest on the ground or on cliffs near the sea. The parent birds forage at sea or on local rubbish heaps and bring back food to the chicks in their nest. On their return to the nest, they stand near one of the chicks and point their beaks to the ground. The chick then pecks the parent's beak, and food is regurgitated for the chick to feed on. It was comparatively easy for Tinbergen and his colleague to investigate what kind of stimulus (short of the natural one) would produce the pecking response in the chicks. A number of stimuli were tried: three-dimensional 'mock-ups' of a gull's head, cardboard cut-outs and even a thin red rod. What appeared to be crucial was the presence of a red spot on the parent's beak. Anything red (the thin red rod, for example) produced the desired pecking response. An otherwise totally life-like mock-up without a red spot produced no response at all. If there was no red spot, the chicks did not peck, the parent bird would not regurgitate and the chicks would starve. This was an experiment. The researchers were deliberately manipulating the IV (the stimulus presented to the chick) in order to observe the pecking response (the DV). The setting, though, was the bird's own nest, a field environment.

Quasi-experiment

Here the setting is a natural one for the participants in the experiment, but instead of the researchers deliberately manipulating the independent variable, changes in the IV occur naturally. It could be argued that it is not an experiment at all because the experimenter does not manipulate the IV. However, the experimenter does take account, in the design of the study, of changes which occur naturally. In this sense, it could be said that the experimenter is deliberately building changes in the independent variable into the experimental design. Namikas and Wehmer (1978) were studying aggression within litters of mice. Male mice which were reared in litters in which they had solely female siblings were more aggressive than those whose litters contained both males and females. Here the independent variable was the composition of the litter. It could vary naturally from one composed entirely of males to one which was entirely female. The dependent variable was the amount of aggressive behaviour observed. The IV varied naturally rather than by deliberate manipulation.

Strengths and weaknesses of experimentation

Strengths

- *Control.* Isolating one or more variables and then manipulating their values to see the effect this has upon another variable makes possible a high degree of control. The experimenter aims to eliminate extraneous variables to concentrate entirely upon the effect that changes in the IV have upon the DV. This can never be totally possible, but control is likely to be greater than in other research methods. Laboratory experiments are likely to be better controlled than field or natural experiments.
- *Cause and effect.* The systematic manipulation of the IV in order to observe the effect of that manipulation on the DV makes it possible to establish a link between cause and effect.
- *Objectivity.* As Popper (1972) has said, it is unrealistic to claim that any observation is totally objective. The experimenter's values, interests, expectations and prejudice will always intrude. Nevertheless, objectivity is a primary aim of scientific study, and it is more nearly realisable with experimentation than with other methods.
- *Replicability.* An experimenter can describe in detail exactly what has been done, and this makes replication easier than in other methods of study. Replication is very important, in that where a study is repeated and similar results obtained, there can be greater confidence in the validity of the theory being tested.
- *The experimenter's control* over such things as when and

where the study should take place, the number and character of the participants and how they should be deployed.

Weaknesses

● *Dehumanisation.* Heather (1976) has claimed that experimentation on human beings treats them rather like machines; it 'depersonalises' and 'dehumanises' them. The use of the word 'subject' is indicative of the attitude taken towards them, and this has consequently now been replaced by the term 'participant' in most cases. This is the term we have employed throughout this book.

> He is regarded as something passive and inert, propelled into action only by the use of some force, either external or internal upon him…Human beings continue to be regarded by psychologists as some kind of helpless clockwork puppet, jerked into life only when something happens to it. (Heather, 1976)

● *Separation from reality.* The controlled and contrived situation of the laboratory experiment is divorced from real life. Claxton (1980) spelled out this divorce. Much of psychology does not:

> deal with whole people but with a very special and bizarre – almost Frankensteinian – preparation, which consists of a brain attached to two eyes, two ears, and two index fingers. This preparation is only to be found inside small gloomy cubicles, outside which red lights burn to warn ordinary people away... It does not feel hungry or tired or inquisitive; it does not think extraneous thoughts or try to understand what is going on. It is, in short, a computer, made in the image of the larger electronic organism that sends it stimuli and records its responses. (Claxton, 1980, p 18)

The impression given that real people behave in the way in which experimental subjects behave may be misleading. For example, no one in real life would be asked to look at a series of lines drawn on a card, compare them with a test line and say which one matches most closely. And yet this was what Asch

(1952), in a classic experiment, asked participants to do. This divorce from reality results in what is termed a lack of **ecological validity**. Validity is discussed fully in Section V.

- *The participant's perception* – how the experiment and the part that participants are asked to play in it are perceived can make a vital difference to the behaviour of participants. They will carefully weigh up the situation and react accordingly. Orne (1962) used the term **demand characteristics** to describe what happens. The participant responds to cues within the experimental situation such as:

1. the physical set-up of the experiment;
2. the experimenter's behaviour; and
3. any clue that might alert the participant to the hypothesis being tested.

Orne and Evans (1965) attempted to explore these effects. A majority of participants (15 out of 18) behaved in ways which were quite alien to them. They were prepared, for example, to pick up a snake which they had been told was poisonous, plunge their hands into a fuming container of what they were told was nitric acid to retrieve a coin and even to throw the 'acid' into the experimenter's face. Outside the experimental situation, they would have been unlikely to do any of these things and, what is more, they suspected no deception. Tedeschi *et al.* (1985) have described this as a 'pact of ignorance'. Thinking that they have caught on to the experimenter's hypothesis, they go along with it, either to save face or so as not to upset the experiment. Whatever the reason, the behaviour of participants may be abnormal and gives a distorted picture of how they would ordinarily behave. Objectivity is compromised.

- The biosocial or physical characteristics of the experimenters (age, sex, race or appearance, for example) may affect the way in which participants react to them.
- There are also factors which have to do with the experimenter's social skills in dealing with participants. They will co-operate more readily with an experimenter who is helpful and friendly.
- *The influence of the participant.* It has been a recurrent criticism of psychological research that participants tend to be

predominantly white, male, American undergraduates. This reflects the ease with which this group can be persuaded to take part. This has been shown to be the case most particularly in social psychology. Tedeschi *et al.* (1985) showed in a survey of research between 1969 and 1979 that 70 per cent of social psychology research projects used college students as participants. Another relevant characteristic of participants in psychological experiments is that they tend to be volunteers. Ora (1965) has found that volunteers are not typical of the population at large. They tend to be more easily influenced, moody, anxious for approval, aggressive and neurotic than are nonvolunteers. Because they are not typical, it is less easy to generalise from them to the whole population.

● *Participants' roles in the research situation.* Weber and Cook (1972) have identified four distinct roles which participants adopt in the research situation:
  – the 'faithful' participant tries to react to the situation as naturally as possible, either deliberately or out of disinterest.
  – the co-operative participant tries to find out the hypothesis being tested in order to help support it.
  – the negativistic participant has the objective of trying to find out the hypothesis to ensure that it is not supported.
  – the apprehensive participant believes that the experimenter is out to find out some hidden truth about him or her. Every effort will be made to avoid negative evaluation.

The use of a **single blind** technique may go some way towards mitigating some of these participant biases. This entails not revealing the purpose of the experiment to participants until after the data have been collected.

The expectations of the experimenter

A further cause of distortion can be the expectations which the experimenter has about the outcome of the experiment. Theory and previous research provide the basis for the hypothesis which is being tested, which is a prediction of the outcome. There is a built-in motive to encourage this to be fulfilled. An experiment conducted by Rosenthal (1966) illustrates this.

Student experimenters were asked to observe rats running through mazes and report their findings. One group was told that their rats were a very bright strain, a second group that their rats were dull. The rats were in fact no different from each other. The results showed that the 'bright' rats had performed much better than the 'dull' ones. Rosenthal discovered three problems relating to the influences exerted by the experimenter:

1. Expectations of the experimenter about what it is predicted will be found may be a source of bias.
2. Good results at the outset of an experiment may produce expectations in the experimenter which are then transmitted to the participants.
3. The interpretation which the researcher puts upon the data will tend to be that which backs up the theory being tested.

A **double blind** technique can be used to mitigate some of these effects. This involves neither the individual administering the experiment nor the participants being aware of the real aims of the experiment until after it is completed.

- *Sampling bias.* Where generalisation needs to be made to a wider group, the sample used has to be typical of that wider group. Where college students are used as participants, they are seen as bright young adults anxious to volunteer, sometimes in return for much-needed payment. Ora's research mentioned above has shown such volunteers to be atypical. Additionally, students are likely to be atypical in that they have a narrower age and intellectual range than nonstudents. While this may be acceptable if the intention of the experimenter is to generalise only to other student volunteers, it is not acceptable to widen this generalisation to those who do not share these characteristics.
- *Statistical inference.* Use is frequently made of statistical inference (see Chapter 3) to enable experimenters to have confidence that their results can be generalised. This makes use of statistical probability. There is nothing at all wrong in this, providing that those who read their work are aware what the use of statistical inference implies. Later chapters in this book will deal in detail with this. At this point, it is sufficient to illustrate the limitations imposed by statistical

inference. It has become customary to employ a criterion of five per cent significance as this provides a balance between the likelihood of a type I or a type II error (see Chapter 1, Section I and Chapter 3, Section II); that is to say, if the statistics show that there is a five in a hundred chance or less that the results obtained could have been due to chance alone, that is held to provide sufficient confidence for the researcher to say that that the effect observed is a real one and not the result of chance. However, there still remains a five per cent probability that there is no real effect at all, that the results *are* in fact due to chance. Hence the need for replication, the repeating of an experiment. When we deal with the writing up of experimental reports (Chapter 5), it will be evident that the main reason for the care taken in reporting is to facilitate replication.

Self-assessment questions

1. Give a brief definition of 'independent variable' and 'dependent variable'.
2. Comment briefly on the strengths and weaknesses of the experimental method.
3. What are meant by 'single blind' and 'double blind' techniques? In what ways can they mitigate bias in experimentation?
4. List some ways in which the use of experimentation makes possible a high degree of control over extraneous variables.

SECTION II EXPERIMENTAL DESIGN AND THE CONTROL OF VARIABLES

So far in this chapter, we have examined experimentation and have seen that control of variables is central to it. In this section, we shall attempt to explain some of the ways in which variables can be controlled in the planning and design stage of a study. In this way, the observations and measurements we make will be more likely to reflect what we are trying to study rather than some extraneous factor which had not been taken into account, that is to say, some **systematic error**. Failure adequately to control these extraneous factors may result in **confounding** of variables. It becomes unclear how much of the difference observed is the result of the conditions being studied, how much is due to (psychological) effects and how much is due to the influence of extraneous variables. To take an example, supposing you were conducting an experiment involving the learning of verbal material under two different conditions, say, in total silence or with background music playing. If all the most intelligent participants operated in one condition and the least intelligent in the other, differences found in learning might well be due not to the conditions in which the learning was taking place, but to the intelligence of the participants. The effect of the independent variable (music or silence) on the dependent variable (learning success) has been **confounded** by a variable with which the experiment is not concerned. There are various experimental designs which may be used to achieve effective control.

Experimental design

Experimental design concerns the decisions which are taken when an experiment is set up. It is principally concerned with the ways in which samples are selected and allocated to **conditions** within an experiment. The term 'condition' relates to the **independent variable (IV)**. This is the variable which an experimenter deliberately manipulates in order to examine the effect of this manipulation on a **dependent variable (DV)**. This is dealt with in the next section.

Related measures design

This is sometimes referred to as repeated measures, and it involves using the same participants in two or more conditions. As with most aspects of design, there are advantages and disadvantages with a related measures design. The advantages are:

● because you are using the same sample twice (or more), you do not need to recruit as many participants; and

- individual differences are not a problem because the same individuals are being tested under each condition.

However, there are disadvantages.

- Order effects are more likely to bias your observations. These include the effects of fatigue or boredom on participants and also practice effects.
- There will clearly be some circumstances in which related measures cannot be used at all. An example might be where participants are asked to memorise something under one condition and then under another. The first memorisation will be bound to interfere with the second. This is likely to be the case even where the material to be memorised is different under each condition. You are introducing yet another source of systematic error – differences in the material memorised.

Independent measures design

An independent measures design involves using different participants for each condition. The advantages and disadvantages of this are the converse of related measures designs.

- You have to recruit more participants because each participant is used under only one condition.
- You run up against the problem of individual differences. Humans are infinitely variable and there may well be differences between the people you recruit which could bias your results.

Matched participants design

This involves identifying what you think are the important differences between individuals which may influence the results of your study. These might include intelligence or ability, gender, age, socioeconomic status or some other factor specific to the study you are doing. Then, against every participant recruited for one condition, another, who has been matched for the characteristics you have identified, is recruited for the other condition. Once pairings have been made, participants are allocated randomly to conditions.

The advantage of this is that, while allowing you to use a separate set of participants for each condition, you are overcoming the problem of individual differences (at least insofar as the characteristics you have identified are concerned).

The disadvantage is the time and expense involved in pretesting for the characteristics which you have decided to match. Besides this, there is always the chance that you failed to identify an individual difference which was in fact a source of systematic error.

Single participant design

You may occasionally choose to select just one participant and test him or her a large number of times under different conditions. For instance, you might test an individual's reaction time to an audible stimulus and compare it with his or her reaction time to a visible one. Clearly, the possibility of generalisation from this kind of study is very limited, but it can be useful as a preliminary to a larger study. For the purpose of statistical analysis, this is treated as though it were an independent measures design.

Order effect

The sequence or order in which events occur in an experiment can bias the results which are obtained. This is most likely to happen when we have opted for a repeated measures design, that is, where the same group of participants are tested under each condition. The experience which participants have when taking part in an investigation is bound to have an effect on them. Suppose that an experiment involves performing a particular task a number of times. The consequences are likely to be that:

● participants get bored or tired performing the same task over and over again. Their responses are unlikely to be as speedy or as accurate on the hundredth as on the first presentation; and
● they also learn how to perform the task better as they go along.

In either case (that of fatigue or boredom, or that of learning), the results are likely to be biased. In order to get over this bias, the experimenter may **counterbalance** the order in which the material is presented. Instead of doing all the tests in Condition A first and then the tests in Condition B, both tests would be divided in half and presented in this order – ABBA. This would hopefully cut out any bias which might result from putting one or the other consistently first.

An alternative strategy to avoid this kind of bias is called **randomisation**. If it were thought that the time of day when the tests were done might have an effect upon the results, then tests under each condition would need to be randomly allocated across all times of the day. It might be done like this. Suppose there are 30 participants, each doing both tests, and the tests go on from 9 am until 5 pm and last an hour. The names of the participants are put on slips and into a 'hat'. The time slots are also put on slips and into a second 'hat'. Each name is drawn randomly and put together with a time slot also randomly drawn (rather like the draw for the FA cup!). Alternatively, a table of random numbers could be used. In this way, it is chance which determines the order in which the tests are done.

Expectations

We have seen in an earlier part of this chapter that expectations, both of participants and of researchers, can have an effect upon the results obtained. As a result, bias may occur as a result of what are termed **demand characteristics**. Reseachers need to make allowance for this at the planning stage.

Single and double blind techniques

One way of doing this is to employ **single** or **double blind** techniques. In a single blind design, the effect of participants' expectations is kept in check by their being unaware, as they complete the tests that make up the research, what the true purpose of the research is. Of course, they could and should be told all about it afterwards. But while the tests are proceeding, they cannot (consciously or unconsciously) influence the results by their expectations of what they feel the 'right' results should be. Similarly, the expectations of researchers may be a source of bias. A double blind technique may be used to control this. In this, neither the persons administering the tests nor the participants are aware of the real purpose of the study and are only carrying out instructions. An illustration will make this clearer.

In an attempt to test the effectiveness of ECT (electroconvulsive therapy) used in the treatment of depression, simulated ECT was used. Procedures were undertaken exactly as in a genuine treatment session, except that no current was used. The doctors who administered the trials were unaware which patients were receiving genuine and which simulated ECT. Patients also were only informed afterwards. Morris and Beck (1974) have reported 146 such double blind studies of ECT and of other drug treatments involving the use of substances used to simulate drugs. In no case was the simulated treatment found to be more effective than the genuine treatment.

Instructions

The instructions which are given to participants can make a great deal of difference. These need to be carefully prepared beforehand so as to ensure that bias does not result from some participants having instructions worded slightly differently from those of others.

Individual differences

It needs to be borne in mind that psychological research is concerned with people and they are infinitely variable. When a researcher uses an independent measures design, that is to say, when different individuals are tested under each condition, the possibility of bias arises from individual differences, particularly in such things as intelligence, personality and socioeconomic status. There are two main ways of mitigating the bias resulting from individual differences:

1. Using a matched participants design, as described earlier. Individuals are pretested for factors which the researchers think are relevant and are then allocated to the conditions in the experiment so that each member of one sample is matched against a member of the other sample.

2. Where there are a large number of participants, the problem of individual differences can be met by randomly allocating participants to each condition.

Self-assessment questions

1. Describe three different experimental designs.
2. What are meant by 'order effects'? How can you mitigate the bias which results from order effects?
3. How is it possible to minimise the bias that results from expectations of:
   (a) researchers; and (b) participants?
4. What precautions should be taken to ensure that bias does not result from the way in which the participants are briefed?

SECTION III   OBSERVATION, SURVEY, CASE STUDY AND INTERVIEW TECHNIQUES

Observation

There will be occasions on which it will not be feasible to intervene in an experimental way to manipulate the independent variable. Alternatives include observation and survey methods. Observation provides first stage data by which hypotheses may be formed. These hypotheses may then be tested experimentally. Clearly, some control is lost and it is no longer possible to infer cause in the same way as in an experiment, but there may be ethical and practical considerations which make experimentation impossible. Ethical issues have been explored in greater detail in Chapter 1. Suffice it to say at this point that ethical considerations might make it difficult, for example, to experiment with a baby's feeding regime. It might prove neither practicable nor ethical to experiment on the effect of teacher attitudes on pupil progress. The attitudes which teachers adopt do not easily lend themselves to manipulation. In such instances, observation of what occurs naturally is likely to be more appropriate. We shall examine three types of observation: **controlled observation**, **naturalistic observation** and **participant observation**.

Controlled observation

This has much in common with experimentation, as well as some of its advantages and disadvantages. It is likely to be carried out in a laboratory in carefully controlled conditions. The main difference will be that there is no manipulation of the variables. The observer simply observes and measures what is there in the situation. Here are two examples:

● Research has been carried out into the effects on behaviour of circadian rhythms. These are naturally occurring cycles of changes in the human body which effect temperature, blood pressure and urine volume, as well as liver, kidney and endocrine gland activity, on a daily cycle. Activity was often found to be three to five times higher during the day than during the night (Luce, 1971). Without manipulating any of these patterns of activity, but by closely observing a large number of individuals, researchers were able to reach some interesting conclusions. One of the projects in Chapter 6 deals with the effects of circadian rhythms on performance on a vigilance task.
● In sleep laboratories, participants are allowed to sleep naturally but with electrodes attached to points on their scalps to measure the electrical activity in the brain by means of an electroencephalogram (EEG). Observations are made in very closely controlled conditions (Hartmann, 1973).

Naturalistic observation

An alternative to controlled observation is **naturalistic observation**. Participants are not brought into a controlled environment, but their spontaneous behaviour is studied in natural surroundings. While this overcomes some of the distortions resulting from an artificial environment, there is some loss of control. This may or may not be a serious matter. Kathy Sylva and her colleagues used naturalistic observation in their study of children's play, carried out in a playgroup in Oxfordshire (Sylva *et al.*, 1980). The design of her study was no less rigorously scientific than an experimental design would have been. Decisions had to be made on what categories of behaviour to observe, at what time intervals data should be recorded, what the important features of the natural setting were and how to minimise the effects on the children's behaviour of being observed.

Another example of naturalistic observation is the study by Ainsworth and Bell (1969). They were interested in the relationship between a mother's responses to her baby and the baby's pattern of crying. The researchers observed 26 babies in their own homes (a natural environment) for four-hour periods at intervals in their first year of life. The independent variables were the promptness with which the mother responded to the baby's crying and the type of response given (picking up or cuddling). The dependent variable was the amount of crying. It was found that during the first three months of life, the babies were more likely to cry when they were alone and least likely to cry when the mother was near or actually holding the child.

Participant observation

A variant on the above is where the researcher actually becomes a part of the group which is being observed. This is designed to minimise the effects on the participants' behaviour of being observed. A classic study of social relationships in a secondary school was carried out by Hargreaves (1967). He was able to observe and report on the attitudes and behaviour of boys and staff at the school by becoming a member of staff for a year.

Another example was that of Whyte (1955), who became a member of an Italian gang in Boston (USA). He took part in all the activities of the gang, including gambling and shady political deals. There are clearly ethical implications here from the point of view of both the deceit involved and also the ethical rightness of engaging in criminal activity to obtain data.

Strengths and weaknesses of observation

Strengths
● There is less chance of the dehumanisation and distortion of which Heather speaks (Section I), as many observational studies are carried out in the field, although this is by no means

always the case. Controlled observation is a case in point.
- Studies of this kind are likely to be more holistic and less reductionist than is often the case with experimental methods. Studies tend to deal with the total situation in which the participants find themselves, rather than with small elements of that situation taken in isolation.
- The great strength of observational studies lies in their ability to provide initial hypotheses on which to base more searching examinations. This forms the basis of the hypothetico-deductive method which forms the core of the scientific approach to knowledge. Figure 5.1 (in Chapter 5, Section I) represents graphically this hypothetico-deductive process, which is cyclical and self perpetuating. This process starts with a theory, perhaps gathered from initial observation, from which an operational hypothesis is deduced, which can be tested and the results of the test used to modify the theory to provide further hypotheses, and so on.

Weaknesses
Some of the weaknesses of the experimental method, mentioned above, apply also to observation.

- *Artificiality*. Laboratory-based observation can be just as artificial as experimentation. Behaviour is equally likely to be distorted. Masters and Johnson (1966) set up a laboratory to study human sexual behaviour by means of controlled observation. It would be hard to show that the sexual behaviour of participants remained unaffected by their being in a laboratory, observed by research workers.
- *Expectancy*. So long as the participants are aware that they are being studied, expectancy effects and demand characteristics may equally be in evidence. By careful design, however, it is possible to minimise the participants' awareness of being observed and the consequent changes in behaviour which this brings about.
- *Sampling bias*. It becomes even more important to ensure that samples observed are typical of the population to which it is intended to generalise the study. This is, however, not always easy to achieve.

Additionally, there are weaknesses which do not apply to experimentation:

● *Cause and effect.* Causality is harder to imply in observational studies. Without manipulating variables, it is harder to pinpoint the cause of effects that are observed. For instance, in Hargreaves' study mentioned above, he observed that lower streams in the school had poorer attitudes towards school, lower attainment and worse behaviour than did higher streams. However, it is hard to attribute this definitively to streaming rather than to a number of other possible causes, socioeconomic conditions or intelligence, for example.

● *Observer bias.* Especially in cases where the structuring of the observations has not been sufficiently careful, there is a danger of observer bias. The flexibility of a less well structured design can lead to subjectivity in what is observed. Even in cases where there has been more careful attention to structuring, the structure itself has been the result of conscious decisions taken by the researcher. It is hard to be certain that value judgments have not entered into the taking of these decisions; in fact, it is almost inevitable that they will. This is not necessarily going to be detrimental, but it does need to be borne in mind when evaluating research.

An example of this kind of bias can be seen in the research of the Polish anthropologist Malinowski (1927). While he was claiming to be a participant observer among the Trobriand islanders, he still continued to live in a separate hut and to regard the islanders as inferior to himself. His 'participant observation' was therefore not truly participant. His theoretical position also was not objective. He started from a Freudian position, examining the extent to which the islanders exhibited aspects of Freudian belief, such as Oedipal conflict. To have been truly unbiased, he would have needed to put his theoretical beliefs to one side, at least until after he had made his observations. The very fact that he was looking for particular kinds of behaviour made it much more likely that he would find it.

Where there is more than one observer, interobserver reliability (see Section V) can be a problem. Care needs to be taken with the instructions that observers are given to ensure that observations are carried out in precisely the same way by all.

Survey method

Another alternative is to use survey methods. Typically, the researcher will assemble a large number of questions to be posed to a representative sample of the relevant population. The questionnaire may be a highly structured one with fixed alternative responses, or more open-ended with respondents able to express themselves more freely. The analysis of the responses is clearly more difficult in the latter case, while in the former there is more scope for the surveyor's own biases to intrude.

An example of the survey method is Rutter's *Fifteen Thousand Hours* (Rutter *et al.*, 1979). The aim was to see how schools differed in academic attainment, attendance and delinquency. The researchers chose 12 schools within a radius of six miles in the Inner London Education Authority area. Survey methods were combined with structured interviews (which might be regarded as oral surveys) and some observation of events in the classroom. Explanatory variables considered included the status and sex composition of the schools' pupils, size and space, age of buildings, the number of sites on which a particular school worked, staffing, class size and school organisation. It was a very well conducted piece of research, but it clearly depended upon a number of value judgments made by the researchers on what variables were likely to prove important.

Strengths and weaknesses of surveys

Strengths

- A major strength of use of surveys is that of economy. A great deal of ground can be covered and responses gained from a large sample comparatively easily. Rutter's study covered 12 schools in Inner London. A large number of factors was examined and the scope of the outcomes was also wide. The researchers were able to obtain data on attendance, pupil behaviour and academic results.
- As with observations, surveys may suggest further areas of research for detailed study by other methods.

Weaknesses

● *Data analysis*. There is always the danger that decisions on what to investigate will be determined not so much by what is important as by what is easy to analyse.

● *Memory failure*. People are frequently questioned in surveys about their past behaviour or practices. It may be difficult for them to be accurate.

● *Distortions*. However carefully interviews and questionnaires are structured, there is always the likelihood that people will not respond truthfully. There several reasons for this, the most important being that:
  – they are simply not sufficiently interested to think carefully about their answers;
  – where responses are made anonymously, there will be a tendency to answer in a way which shows the respondent up in the best light;
  – the wording of written questions or the use of nonverbal cues, tone of voice and so on by interviewers may influence responses;
  – there may be several interviewers, each with his or her own set of biases.

● *Design difficulties*. There are problems both with closely structured and with open-ended questionnaires. Where the questionnaire is highly structured, the preconceptions of the compiler will show through and might force respondents to answer in a way which does not entirely reflect their views. On the other hand, where the survey is more open-ended, this may bring problems of subjectivity in the way in which responses are interpreted.

● *Response and behaviour mismatches*. Responses to questions about behaviour, both verbal and written, may not reflect what people actually do. What they do may vary considerably from what they say they do.

Case study method

The methods we have so far examined have been **nomothetic** ones. They depend upon the scientific observation of a number of participants and attempt to arrive at principles of behaviour which apply to all of them and which may be generalised to a wider population. The alternative view to take is that human beings are essentially unique individuals and it is this uniqueness, more than what is common among them, which is worthy of study. This is the **idiographic** approach to the study of behaviour. It is not appropriate in this section to deal at length with the merits of idiographic or nomothetic approaches to the study of behaviour. There is a full discussion of this in *Perspectives in Psychology* (Malim *et al.*, 1992, pp 70–6). Case study is different from experiment, observation and survey in two major respects:

1. It is essentially idiographic in that it involves making a detailed study of single individuals or instances of something, a family, for example.
2. It tends to depend more upon **qualitative** rather than **quantitative** analysis, that is to say, upon a verbal description of participants more than upon numerical analysis of features of their behaviour. While numerical measurement of characteristics is not excluded, the emphasis is upon description more than upon measurement.

Case study methods have been fairly extensively used in psychology. Among the most well-known users of the method was Freud. Freud and other psycholanalysts employed case study in their compilation of detailed case histories of the patients they treated. It was from these case histories that their theories of personality were derived. The case of Little Hans illustrates this. Hans was the son of one of Freud's friends, a doctor interested in Freud's work. He developed a phobia of horses and was especially terrified of being bitten by one of them. Freud's interpretation was that in Hans' unconscious mind he harboured incestuous desires for his mother but was afraid that his father would find out and castrate him as a punishment. On a conscious level, he expressed his anxiety in the form of a fear of horses, which symbolised his father, and of biting, which symbolised castration. This explanation was backed up by detailed evidence. Hans particularly feared white horses with blinkers and black round the mouth. His father had a black moustache and sometimes wore glasses. Furthermore, Hans' father sometimes played 'horses' with his son, always as the horse with Hans as the rider. All these data were carefully collected to support Freud's explanation of the phobia. More generally also, the data provided support for the general thesis that boys in the so-called *phallic* stage suffered from Oedipal conflict (so called after Oedipus, a figure in Greek mythology). This was characterised by the boy's sexual attraction to his mother and fear of his father's vengeance.

Strengths and weaknesses of case study

Strengths
- Case study allows detailed study of all aspects of an individual case rather than just being concerned with a few measurable characteristics. There is a greater chance that insights might be gained into the nature of behaviour, which might well be missed in other methods of study.
- Case study is based more upon description and upon qualitative data, than upon measurement. It is therefore less likely to ignore those facets of behaviour which cannot easily be measured.

Weaknesses
- *Generalisation.* Because case study method deals with only one, or possibly a very few, individuals studied in great depth, it is not as easy to generalise findings to other people. The results of a study of one individual are really only valid in the case of that individual. Great caution should be exercised in generalising to others.
- *Subjectivity.* Because they are based upon the analysis of qualitative rather than quantitative data, interpretation is in the hands of researchers alone. They also are responsible for deciding what to include in their descriptions and what to leave out. This makes it very easy for the researcher to leave out what does not support his or her theory. For instance, Freud was the sole analyst, observer and interpreter of what he observed in his patients. It was open to him to interpret what he observed in a way which would support his ideas about Oedipal conflict at this particular stage in a boy's development.

Interview techniques

Interviews used in psychological research may vary from those which are tightly scripted and used in conjunction with other survey methods (as in Rutter's study, mentioned above) to free discussion between interviewer and interviewee. Massarik (1981) listed six types of interview:

1. *Hostile interview.* In this case, the two parties have different goals. It might, for instance be a police interrogation in which the suspect is trying to limit the amount of information which is elicited, while the interrogator is trying to gain as much information as possible.
2. *The survey interview.* This might be, for example the kind of interview which ensues when you are stopped on the street by a market researcher. There is little personal involvement on either side. This very lack of personal involvement leads to objectivity.
3. *The rapport interview.* This might be, for example, the kind of interview which takes place when a prospective student applies for a place at college. The goals and boundaries are fairly well defined, and the format is usually laid down beforehand (at least in framework). However, within these limits there is a high degree of interaction, and the interviewer will attempt to establish a rapport with the interviewee. Both are co-operating to reach a single goal (perhaps the right choice of course for the prospective student).
4. *The asymmetrical trust interview.* In this kind of interview, there is one party who is more trustful than the other. Very frequently, this is a matter of superior knowledge and skill. In a doctor–patient interview, the patient is likely to have a high level of trust in the doctor, which may or may not be matched by the doctor's trust in the patient.
5. *The depth interview.* In this kind of interview, common in psychological research, the intention of the interviewer is to establish the greatest possible trust and rapport with the interviewee in order to explore views and motivations in some depth.
6. *The phenomenological interview.* There are few boundaries or limitations in this kind of interview. It often amounts to an open-ended discussion and depends upon trust and caring.

Some examples of interviews in use

Lynch (1960) was exploring the 'cognitive maps' which individuals held of their cities, that is to say, the representation they held of them in their minds. Participants were asked to describe a journey from one part of the city to another. Lynch found that individuals paid special attention to distinctive features and that these were not the same in each case. There were also blank areas of the town which they were not able to describe at all. This approach would be described under Massarik's categorisation as 'rapport interviewing'.

Kadushin (1976) was interested in parents who had adopted older children (older than five years). He interviewed the parents of 91 such families and derived, from transcripts of the interviews, measures of parental satisfaction. In a large number of cases (between 82 and 87 per cent), there was a high level of satisfaction. Children had developed close relationships with their adoptive parents and showed little sign of the earlier abuse they had suffered. This would be described under Massarik's categorisation as 'depth interviewing'.

Interviews are frequently employed in conjunction with other methods and suffer many of the same strengths and weaknesses as survey techniques. A great deal of information may be obtained comparatively easily, although it is much more expensive in terms of manpower. There is also the problem of data analysis, especially in those kinds of interview which are most open-ended. There always has to be a compromise between the maximisation of the information gained and the ease with which it may be analysed.

Ethogenics

Harré (1979) suggested that small units of human behaviour, particular acts or actions, were inappropriate as the focus for the study of social behaviour, and that researchers should take episodes rather than individual acts or actions as the unit of study. People, he argued, experience life as a series of episodes, rather like scenes in a play. He also proposed that it was likely to be more meaningful to study people's own accounts of their experiences rather than just looking at their behaviour from outside. This was termed **account analysis**. This was not entirely new. In fact, it goes back to the importance placed upon introspection in the early days of psychology. But what Harré suggested was that it should be used as a valid technique for investigation rather than a last resort when there was no other method available. For example, Marsh *et al.* (1978), studying the behaviour of football crowds, used ethogenic methods to discover that deindividuation (the loss of individuality when people become members of a large crowd) was much less than had been thought. A further example of **ethogenic methods** in use is **discourse analysis**, the study of the way in which people express themselves to obtain insights into, for example, social assumptions. It may reveal racist assumptions, for example, which may not be revealed equally well by looking at acts or actions.

Popper (1972) has said that the criteria for *scientific* study is that it should be **objective**, **generalisable**, **accessible** and **refutable**. By these criteria, it is difficult to claim that material obtained through some of these methods is scientific.

Self-assessment questions

1. What are the major respects in which observation differs from experimentation?
2. List some of the strengths and weaknesses of observation.
3. What is meant by (a)'controlled observation'; and (b)'participant observation'?
4. List the weaknesses of survey methods.
5. List six types of interview. Which of these are the most open-ended, which the most structured? Identify their usefulness in psychological investigation.

SECTION IV   CORRELATIONAL DESIGNS

It is appropriate to discuss **correlation** at this point. It is not a method of study in the same way that experimentation or observation are, but rather a statistical technique. It is widely used to measure the extent to which two variables are related to one another. For instance, a researcher may be interested in whether there is any truth in the suggestion that those who are gifted musically are also likely to be good at mathematics. Or whether those who are creative are also intelligent. Correlation can indicate the degree of relationship which exists in a group of people between one aspect of their behaviour and another.

In practice, correlation operates like this. A researcher sets out to discover whether there is any relationship between one aspect of behaviour and another. For instance, it might be useful to find out whether tests of intelligence and of creative ability were in fact measuring the same thing. A group of participants might be tested, using tests of both intelligence and creativity. A test of correlation would indicate the degree to which the two sets of measurements were related. What is being measured is the degree to which the two sets of measurements vary in harmony with each other. This measure is known as a **coefficient of co-variance** or a **correlation coefficient**.

Further detail about the ways in which correlation may be expressed and the ways in which correlation coefficients are calculated can be found in Chapters 3 and 4.

Some examples of correlation in psychological research

Here are two examples of the use of correlation:

1. Hill *et al.* (1976) set out to test the extent to which people were attracted to those like themselves. They measured the ages, educational attainment, attractiveness and attitudes of 200 couples who were going out together but who had not yet made any formal commitment to one another. On each of these measures, correlations were carried out between the couples. Those who remained together to get engaged or married tended to be more alike on these measures than did those whose relationships ended within the next year.

2. Rushton (1978) set out to explore whether people living in small towns were likely to be more helpful than those in big cities. Questions such as 'Do you have change for the telephone?' or 'Can you tell me the time?' were asked of individuals in a variety of locations, both small and large. The degree of helpfulness was correlated with the size of the location. People in suburbs or small towns were found to be more likely to be helpful than those in big cities. There was a

negative correlation between the size of the location and the helpfulness of the people. As will be fully explained in Chapter 3, a negative correlation indicates that there is an inverse relationship between the two measurements (in this case, the smaller the community, the greater likelihood of people being helpful to strangers). The strength of this relationship is indicated by the correlation coefficient. A zero coefficient shows that there is no relationship at all, a correlation of 1 (either + or –) that there is a perfect match. Values between these extremes are expressed as decimal fractions.

Strengths and weaknesses of correlation

Strengths

- *Detecting relationships.* Correlation is valuable in that it is possible to identify the direction and strength of a relationship between two (or more) variables. It allows an investigator to measure relationships between variables without manipulating or controlling them.

- *Making predictions.* If we know that there is a high correlation between two variables, it becomes possible (with some caution) to predict the probable value of one variable if we know the value of the other. For example, supposing that a high negative correlation was found between the hours spent watching TV and the grades attained by students in the end of term exams, you could predict that a compulsive TV viewer would probably not achieve high grades. It is important to note that this does not imply that TV watching *causes* low grades. There could easily be a third variable affecting both – lack of interest in the subject, perhaps. If you have a perfect relationship (that is, a correlation of +1 or −1), you can make your predictions with absolute certainty. But this does not often happen. With imperfect relationships, this certainty becomes a probability. This probability is related to:
  - the number of pairs of scores; and
  - the size of the correlation.

- *Assessing the independence of concepts.* It is valuable to use correlation to assess whether or not the ideas we are examining are distinct and separate, or whether they are simply facets of the same thing. For example, Witkin *et al.* (1962) developed the concept of field dependence or independence, that is, the ability to analyse a problem distinctly from its context. Field independence was, he claimed, a human characteristic quite separate and distinct from intelligence. In support of this claim, he reported correlational analyses of children's scores on tests of field independence and intelligence test scores taken from the Wechsler Intelligence Scale for Children (WISC). The low correlations which he found showed that there was no significant relationship between the two measures; they were not measuring the same thing. Other researchers, however, have found high correlations between these two measures, indicating that they were measuring at least some of the same characteristics.

Weaknesses
- *Correlation and cause.* As has already been indicated, it is very important to stress that correlation does not imply cause. There may be several variables which are interrelated, and it is difficult to know whether the two chosen for comparison are related by cause and effect. In Hill *et al.*'s study, mentioned above, similarity to one another is only one of the things which might have affected the durability and success of relationships. The amount of time the couples were able to spend together could equally well have been a factor.
- *Extrapolation.* It is often tempting to extrapolate from the findings of a correlational study. We must keep within the limits of the data that have been collected. For example, suppose it has been found that there is a strong relationship (a high positive correlation) between the length of time spent on homework and success in examinations, and the length of time spent on homework varied between half an hour and three hours, while the measure of success varied between one and six GCSE passes. It would be quite erroneous to suggest that if children spent five hours a night on homework, they would be likely to get 10 GCSE passes.

Self-assessment questions

1. Explain how correlation can help us to assess whether a concept (intelligence, for example) is separate and distinct from another (say, creative ability).
2. Why is it not possible to infer cause from correlation?
3. Explain how the use of correlational techniques may help us to be able to predict behaviour.

SECTION V   SOME FURTHER IMPORTANT CONSIDERATIONS IN RESEARCH

Important factors included in this section include reliability, validity and standardisation.

Reliability

It is very important that any test which is used in a piece of research should be **reliable**. That is to say, it should not be like an elastic tape measure, measuring differently depending on how hard you pull it! Every time a test is used, researchers need to be certain that the measures obtained accurately reflect real phenomena. This consistency in measurement may be of several kinds:

1. *Internal consistency.* A test needs to be consistent in content. If some parts of a test produce markedly different results from others as a measure of the same phenomenon, then the test is flawed. Accordingly, it is common practice to employ a **split-half** test of reliability. The scores obtained from a sizeable sample of people are divided into two. Scores from odd-numbered items are correlated against scores obtained from even-numbered items. You would expect, with a reliable test, a correlation of +0.8 or +0.9 with a large sample. You can easily see that dividing a test in this way is preferable to comparing, say, the first half and the second half of the test. Boredom, fatigue and learning are likely to confound your results. Besides, it is often the case that a test will start with easier items and and become progressively more difficult.

2. *Consistency over time*. It is important that a test measures the same every time it is applied. It will be of no use if results vary wildly each time the test is used even though the participants are very similar. To check this reliability over time, a **test–retest** technique can be used. A sample of participants is tested twice using the same test, with perhaps a month's interval between tests. Results from the two tests are correlated, and it would be expected that a good test would yield a very high correlation – (perhaps +0.8 or +0.9).

Sometimes this kind of test-retest is not really feasible. Too much learning might occur as the test is done the first time, and this would bias the results. In such cases, a different but parallel form of the test might be used on each occasion. Eysenck and Eysenck (1964) produced two parallel forms of their Personality Inventory for this reason.

Intertester reliability

Yet another question of reliability occurs when more than one researcher is involved in the testing of participants in a study. It is clearly necessary for the way in which the test is carried out to be precisely the same whichever researcher is carrying out the test. There is a need for very explicit instructions and the establishment in advance of clear criteria for judgments which are made. An obvious case for intertester reliability occurs when public examinations are conducted and there are a number of examiners. Before the examining commences, there is a co-ordination meeting at which the criteria for the award of marks are clearly established. Then as the marking progresses, samples are withdrawn for scrutiny by the Chief Examiner to ensure that intertest reliability is maintained. It is also possible to correlate the results of one tester's work against that of another to ensure that there is harmony between them. In a well-conducted test, there should be a very high correlation between testers.

Validity

A second issue rests on whether the test a researcher employs actually measures what it is claimed that it measures. This is the issue of **validity**. There has been some controversy about whether GCSE examiners should award marks for English, spelling and punctuation in subjects other than English. It is evident that if they do, they are no longer just testing History, Geography or whatever, they are testing English spelling and grammar as well. Their validity as tests of History or Geography will have been compromised.

The type of validity which needs to be tested depends upon what the test is for. The following are frequently assessed:

● face validity
● predictive validity
● content validity
● concurrent validity
● construct validity
● ecological validity
● experimental validity.

Face validity

A test needs to look as though it tests what it says it tests. An aptitude test for secretaries which involved their speed in climbing ladders would not have good face validity but, of course, it would as a test for firefighters.

Predictive validity

A test can be used to predict what might occur in the future. For example, it might be possible to construct an aptitude test for driving. This should assess the likelihood of success *before* a course of driving instruction. How valid this test is depends upon how well the results from it correlate with success in the subsequent driving test. A test which has been validitated in this way can then be used to make an assessment of how good the course of instruction is. If the test is known to be valid and if many people who have been assessed as having a high aptitude for driving then go on to fail the driving test, the driving instructor could perhaps do better.

Content validity

Content validity relates to testing those skills necessary for good performance. A test of agility might have good content validity in a test for ballet dancers, for instance, while a mental arithmetic test would not.

Concurrent validity

This is perhaps the most useful kind of validity. When there already exists a well-established test for some characteristic, the results of a test produced ostensibly for the same thing ought to correlate highly with it if it is to be considered to be valid. A correlation of +0.8 or +0.9 might be expected between the two measures with a large sample. To take an example of this, when 11+ 'intelligence' tests were widely used, their concurrent validity was frequently assessed by making comparisons between results on these tests and on school achievement tests in English and Mathematics, the assumption being that intelligent children would be likely to do well in both.

Construct validity

Construct validity relates to the accuracy with which a test measures the psychological construct which it is set up to measure. When there is not total agreement between testmakers about the definition of the psychological construct to be measured, construct validity become very difficult to achieve. There have been many tests of creative ability constructed, for example, without any very clear consensus on what creativity amounts to. One way of assessing the construct validity of a test is to match it with other manifestations of the construct in question. People who are generally acknowledged to be 'creative' ought to do well on a creativity test if that is to be seen as having construct validity.

Ecological validity

Ecological validity relates to the extent to which the context in which something is being investigated relates to what is found in the 'real world'. For example, there has been a great deal of research into memory which consists of participants attempting to memorise lists of words. This has nothing whatever to say to us about remembering when Aunt Jane's birthday is; it may have little **ecological validity**. Neisser (1982) had this to say:

> You need only tell a friend, not himself a psychologist, that you study memory. Given a little encouragement, your friend will describe all sorts of interesting phenomena; the limitations of his memory for early childhood, his inability to remember appointments, his aunt who could recite poems from memory by the hour, the regrettable decline in his ability to remember names, how well he could find his way round his home town after thirty years' absence, the difference between his memory and someone else's. Our research has almost nothing to say about any of these topics. (Neisser 1982)

What Neisser is saying is that memory research, as presently conducted, has poor ecological validity.

Experimental validity

This can be closely related to the above. **External experimental validity** relates to the extent to which the experimental situation represent situations that occur in everyday life. Excessive reliance upon students as participants, for example, distorts the validity of experimentation by removing it from the ambit of the 'man in the street'. Sears (1986) has claimed that this has a distorting influence on the understanding of human behaviour. Researchers need to study different people in different situations if they are to understand the full range of human experience. **Internal experimental validity** relates to such things as demand characteristics (discussed earlier) or evaluation apprehension (the way in which the very fact that an individual is being observed or tested alters his or her behaviour). Both internal and external experimental validity need to be considered. When they are lacking, the investigation is likely to be compromised.

Standardisation

In order to make fair comparisons between sets of data, you need to compare like with like. When a measuring instrument is calibrated, norms are established as criteria for measurement. A thermometer is calibrated so that the point at which water freezes is zero on the centigrade scale and the point at which it boils is 100 degrees. Similarly, with psychological or scholastic tests, some objective criterion needs to be established. If a child comes home from school, boasting that he got 70 per cent in his maths test, it means very little until norms have been established. It may have been a very easy test on which the average mark was 95 per cent. On the other hand, it might have been a test where the average mark was 35 per cent, so that 70 is exceptionally good. Without some standardisation, you just do not know. To obtain a **norm**, a criterion against which to measure any particular score on a test, it is necessary to test a large representative sample of the group for which the test is intended. The hope is to obtain a **normal distribution** of scores, a symmetrical distribution in which the largest number of scores cluster round the mean (the arithmetical average). This is also known as a **Gaussian curve**. The characteristics of this normal distribution are known, so that comparisons can easily be made whenever the test is used. For example, it is known that 68.26 per cent of all the scores in such a distribution fall within one **standard deviation** of the mean and that 95.44 per cent fall within two standard deviations of the mean (a standard deviation is a measurement of how widely dispersed the scores are. It will be fully discussed in Chapter 3). It is therefore possible to make an estimate of how likely it is for any particular score to occur.

An example might make this clearer. If a representative sample against which comparisons are to be made has a mean score of 50 per cent and a standard deviation of 10, then the score of 70 per cent is two standard deviations above the mean. Two standard deviations from the mean include 95.44 of the scores; what is left amounts to 4.56 per cent, and that is divided between the highest scores and the lowest, between both ends of the curve. We are only interested in the top end (that is, the top 2.28 per cent). As our score of 70 per cent falls two standard deviations above the mean, the chance of a score as high or higher than this happening is 2.28 per cent.

z scores

It is possible to express any score as a number of standard deviations above or below the mean. A mean score of 50 would be zero, one of 55 would be +0.5 and one of 45 would be –0.5 (one standard deviation, remember, is 10, half a standard deviation [0.5] is 5). These are known as z scores. It is possible to work out the probability (p) that any particular z score has of occurring; a table of the probability of z scores is included at the end of this book (Appendix III, Table B).

Standard scores

It may be inconvenient to express scores as plus or minus decimal fractions, which is what z scores must inevitably be, so they are frequently converted into something easier and more meaningful. One of the most commonly found **standard scores** is a quotient. Quotients assume a mean of 100 and a standard deviation of 15, and are the normal means of expressing intelligence scores. To convert a z score into a quotient, start with the mean (100) and add or subtract 15 times the z score (the formula is $100 \pm 15z$).

Self-assessment questions

1. Why should we wish to measure the psychological characteristics of individuals? What criteria will be likely to determine a measurement's usefulness?
2. What are meant by 'reliability' and 'validity' in relation to psychological testing? How can you ensure that a test is reliable and valid?
3. What do you mean when you say that an investigation is likely to yield 'ecologically valid' data?
4. Why is it necessary to standardise scores? Explain what are meant by 'z scores' and 'quotients'.

FURTHER READING

Malim T., Birch A. and Wadeley A. (1992) *Perspectives in Psychology* (Basingstoke, Macmillan)

Mean .. Median .. Mode .. they're all well below average.

Presenting the Results 3

At the end of this chapter you should be able to:

1. appreciate the value of effective descriptive and inferential statistics when presenting the results of a study;
2. produce a variety of descriptive statistics designed to describe and summarise data;
3. understand the purposes of inferential statistics in relation to the use of probability and significance testing;
4. understand the principles underlying correlational analyses; and
5. choose appropriate significance tests to analyse data drawn from your own practical investigations.

INTRODUCTION

There are many different ways of presenting and interpreting the data from a psychological investigation. All of them involve the use of statistics, and this chapter is about helping to make you familiar with a range of statistical techniques that can be used to describe and analyse data.

Many students of psychology approach statistics with a fair amount of fear and misgiving. Therefore, this chapter is also about helping you to realise the following:

- Statistics are a very useful tool which can help you to describe and make sense of the data you collect in your practical work.

● It is not necessary for you to be a mathematical genius in order to use a wide range of statistical procedures. The basic techniques for displaying your data are straightforward and easily used – most of them you will already have encountered at school and in everyday life.

● Statistics that are used to analyse and assess your data do not involve complicated mathematical procedures or committing long, involved formulae to memory. The tests are available in textbooks such as this one and can be applied in much the same way as if you were following a recipe to make a cake.

There are two main kinds of statistics:

● **Descriptive statistics** are used to describe or summarise your data, for example producing a bar chart or calculating an average such as the mean.

● **Inferential statistics** are used to help us to draw conclusions – make inferences – about the data collected in a study.

Sections I and II will deal with descriptive and inferential statistics respectively.

Before looking in more detail at these two types of statistics, it is important to know something about different kinds of data or **levels of measurement**.

Levels of measurement

There are several ways of measuring what is observed in an investigation. At the simplest level, you can just count the number of events that occur (nominal data); you may wish to record the rank order of things (ordinal data) or measure more precisely using various different instruments, such as a ruler or clock (interval/ratio data). Let us examine these in more detail.

● *Nominal data*
  Where you wish to categorise something and then to count the number of times something falls into this category, you will be using nominal data. For example, a researcher observing the incidence of aggression in children will

probably identify clearly what is meant by an incident of aggression and then go on to count how many of such events occur within a particular space of time and in the particular conditions which are being investigated. This is known as nominal, categorical or frequency measurement.

Where you use numbers (or other identifying features such as letters) simply as labels, this is also considered to be nominal data. Examples of this are the numbers on a footballer's shirt or those used to identify a train or bus.

- *Ordinal data*

  At a slightly more sophisticated level, it is possible to rank events which are observed in order – first, second, third, and so on. This is ordinal measurement. Without accurately measuring the times taken by a group of runners to complete a course, it is still possible to put them in order – 1st, 2nd...54th. This form of measurement tells you something about the participants in the race beyond merely counting them, but at the same time it gives no indication of the differences between them. The runner who finished first may have finished in 59 minutes, the second in 60 minutes and the third in 70 minutes, but with their performance measured in this way (ordinally) no account is taken of these variations. So the amount of information conveyed, while more than with the nominal scale, is still less than with an interval or ratio scale of measurement.

- *Interval or ratio data*

  To use the same example, if the organisers of the race timed in minutes how long each of the competitors took to complete the course, they would be employing a ratio scale of measurement. There is a defined difference in the performance of the runners. Each unit of measurement (a minute) is the same in terms of what it represents as is every other one. The difference between runner 2's and runner 3's performance is ten times as great as that between runners 1 and 2.

  There is just one difference between interval and ratio scales. Ratio data involve a true zero point, whereas zero on an interval scale is purely arbitrary. With measurements such as that of time in seconds or distance in feet, 0 means no time or no distance, since these are ratio scales with clearly defined points of measurement. It is quite in order to say that a measurement of 4 feet is twice as long as one of two feet. However, this is not the case with an interval scale. A commonly used example of interval scales are temperature as measured by the Celsius and Fahrenheit scales. Zero on both these scales does not mean 'no temperature'. Only the Kelvin scale has a true zero and can therefore be classed as a ratio scale.

Despite this difference between them, it is important to note, that for statistical purposes, interval and ratio data are treated in exactly the same way.

Some distinctions between levels of measurement

- Levels of measurement are hierarchical. That is to say, each level includes those below it. Ratio measurement includes all the characteristics of interval measurement and adds a fixed zero point. Interval scores include information about order and add to this measurement of the intervals between ranks. Ordinal measurement includes information about numbers in each category and adds to this a rank order. The lowest of the scales of measurement, nominal, simply counts events.

- You can always convert scales of measurement downwards. An interval scale of measurement can easily be converted to ordinal by ranking scores, but some information is lost. If there is doubt about the accuracy of your measurement, it might be advisable to downgrade the level of measurement in this way. If you establish categories for the runners in the race, say those who finish in the first hour, in the first hour and a half and in the first two hours, then you might have 1 finisher in the first category, 17 in the second and 35 in the third. This is nominal measurement and again there has been some information lost.

SECTION I   DESCRIPTIVE STATISTICS

Remember that descriptive statistics aim to describe or summarise the data you may have collected in a practical exercise. If descriptive statistics are used well, they will present your results clearly and in a way that can be readily understood by a reader. Box 3.1 lists the range of descriptive statistics which will be discussed in this section.

BOX 3.1 *KINDS OF DESCRIPTIVE STATISTICS*		
Tables	**Measures**	**Graphics**
Frequency tables	Dispersion	Bar charts
	Range | Standard	
Tables of raw scores	deviation	Histograms
Tables of summary scores	Central tendency	Graphs
	Mean | Median | Mode	Pie charts
Frequency distribution tables	Correlation coefficients	Scattergrams
Tables of ranked scores		Frequency polygons

It might be helpful to start with a brief note on some of the symbols which you are likely to meet:

Σ Add together

N   The number of items/scores

D   Difference

X   Score

For example:

$\dfrac{\Sigma X}{N}$ means add the scores together and divide by the number of scores

Measures of central tendency

It is often useful to have one single measure – a typical or repre-sentative score – which will summarise a set of scores. There are three key **measures of central tendency** (or averages) as follows.

The **mean,** or arithmetic average, is arrived at by adding together all the scores and dividing the result by the number of scores, for example:

$$9 + 7 + 8 + 5 + 6 = 35 \qquad \text{Mean} = \frac{35}{5} = 7$$

The formula for the mean is $\dfrac{\Sigma X}{N}$

The **median** is a value which has as many scores above it as below. It can be found by listing the scores in order of size and identifying the middle one, for example:

2 3 3 5 7 9 13   or   2 3 4 5 6 8 11 14

median = 5   median = 5.5

(Because there is an even number of scores, an average has been taken of the two middle scores, 5 and 6)

The **mode** is the most frequently occurring value. It is useful to gain a general impression of the average where there is a large set of numbers, for example:

5 4 5 9 8 5 7 5 8 6 3 4 5   Mode = 5

Which measure should I use?

The mean is the preferred average because:

● it makes use of all the scores and the total; and
● it can be used in other, more advanced, mathematical analyses such as calculating a standard deviation (see Box 3.3).

The mean is useful where scores are fairly evenly distributed about the central value. However, if there are a few very atypical scores, the mean might give a misleading picture of the typical value. Therefore, the median or mode should be used.

■ **EXERCISE 3.1**

Work out the mean and the median of the following sets of scores and then decide which measure is the more representative of the set.

(a) 76 77 78 78 79 80   (b) 1 3 76 77 78 78 79 80

Answers at the end of the section.

Table of raw scores

This involves simply listing the scores drawn from a practical exercise. Imagine you are carrying out an experiment to test out a new memorising aid you have devised. A way of doing this might be:

- First, draw a sample of people who are as representative as possible of the population in which you are interested, say college students aged 17–19 (see Chapter 1 for a discussion of populations and samples).
- It would be sensible to compare the performance of a group who made use of the memory aid (the experimental group) with a group who had used a conventional memorising technique. Therefore, the participants could be randomly allocated to two conditions, A and B. In Condition A, participants would be given a memorising task, for example a list of 20 nonsense syllables, and would use the new memory aid. In Condition B, the participants would be given the same memorising task but would be asked to use a conventional technique.
- The dependent variable would be the results of the memorising task – the number of correct syllables recalled; the independent variable would be the use or non-use of the special memorising technique. Of course, you would need carefully to control as many extraneous variables as possible (see Chapter 2, Section II).

The data you collect might look something like that in Figure 3.1.

Ranked scores

You might also wish to show the relationship between the scores by indicating who scored highest, lowest, and so on. If so, columns can be added in which you indicate the rankings as in Figure 3.1. You will see from Figure 3.1 that participant 1 recalled the greatest number of syllables and participant 21 the least (see Box 3.2 for a description of how to rank data).

Frequency tables

Another kind of table might simply illustrate the number of times a particular event occurred. This would be a table of **frequencies**. An example might be a table to show how many females scored at a particular level compared with the number of males. If in the data in Table 3.1, we assume that participants 1–10 and 21–30 are females and the rest males, a table of frequencies to indicate the number of males and females scoring more than 10 would be as in Figure 3.2.

Bar charts and pie charts

Both of these can be used to give an instant graphical representation of the results of a study.

Figure 3.3(a) represents a summary of the data from the memory experiment previously described, in the form of bar charts. You would first need to work out the mean of the scores for each condition.

FIGURE 3.1
Table of raw scores showing number of nonsense syllables correctly recalled

Condition A (with memory aid)			Condition B (without memory aid)		
Participant	Raw scores	Ranked scores	Participant	Raw scores	Ranked scores
1	15	40	21	5	1
2	11	19	22	12	25.5
3	12	25.5	23	13	32.5
4	13	32.5	24	10	13.5
5	10	13.5	25	7	3
6	14	37.5	26	9	8
7	12	25.5	27	10	13.5
8	13	32.5	28	12	25.5
9	9	8	29	8	4.5
10	11	19	30	6	2
11	13	32.5	31	10	13.5
12	14	37.5	32	9	8
13	12	25.5	33	14	37.5
14	12	25.5	34	8	4.5
15	10	13.5	35	11	19
16	11	19	36	9	8
17	13	32.5	37	11	19
18	9	8	38	13	32.5
19	12	25.5	39	10	13.5
20	14	37.5	40	12	24.5

This kind of table lists each individual participant's raw score. Note that the labelling of the table is as important as its contents.

BOX 3.2   PROCEDURE FOR RANKING DATA

If you have to rank a set of scores, it is helpful to do this on a spare sheet of paper.

Procedure

Place all the scores in order of size with the smallest first. For example:

3, 5, 6, 7, 8, 10, 12, 15

Below each score, place the rank, giving the lowest score rank 1, the next lowest rank 2 and so on. For example:

Score	3	5	6	7	8	10	12	15
Rank score	1	2	3	4	5	6	7	8

Suppose you have data for which some of the scores are the same. For example:

7, 9, 9, 12, 14, 15, 15, 15, 18, 20

In this case, the scores which are the same, known as tied scores, must *share* a rank. For example:

Score	7	9	9	12	14	15	15	15	18	20
Rank score	1	2.5	2.5	4	5	7	7	7	9	10

Note that the two 9s would take up ranks 2 and 3. Therefore, the allocated rank is calculated by adding together 2 and 3 and then dividing by 2: 2 + 3 = 5, divided by 2 = 2.5.

This procedure always applies where you have an *equal* number of tied scores – add together the ranks that would be taken up and then divide by the number of ranks.

The three 15s would take up ranks 6, 7 and 8. Therefore, the allocated rank is 7, the middle one. (Note that the next highest number, 18, then receives the rank 9.)

This procedure applies whenever you have an *unequal* number of tied scores. Look to see which ranks would be taken up by the scores and then allocate the middle one to your tied scores.

NB: Some of the statistical tests described in Chapter 4 require you to rank the data before the test is applied. To do this, you would use the above procedure.

FIGURE 3.2
Frequency table showing number of males and females scoring higher than 10 in a memorising task

	Condition A (with the aid)	Condition B (without the aid)
Males	8	5
Females	8	3

FIGURE 3.3
Bar chart showing mean number of nonsense syllables correctly recalled

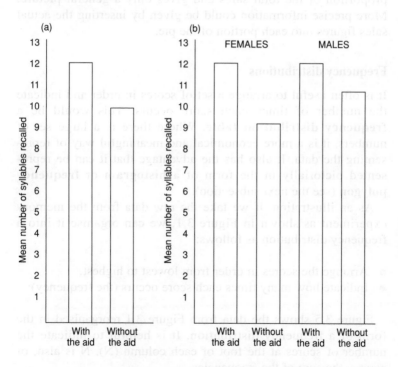

Note that the DV (syllables recalled) goes on the vertical axis; the horizontal axis represents the IV (with or without the aid); the bars represent the mean scores for each of the two conditions.

You could of course also represent the mean scores for males and females separately in the two conditions; it would look like Figure 3.3(b).

The data in Figure 3.2 could be displayed in the form of a pie chart (so called because of its shape), as in Figure 3.4(a).

Note that where you are comparing scores drawn from two different conditions as in Figure 3.4(a), a pie chart would not give such an immediate and clear picture as would a bar chart. A pie chart is perhaps more useful for giving a general picture of the proportions of something such as sales of particular commodities. An illustration of this in relation to a fictitious manufacturing company can be seen in Figure 3.4(b). Each section represents a proportion of the total sales and gives only a general picture. More precise information could be given by inserting the actual sales figures into each portion of the pie.

Frequency distributions

It is often useful to arrange a set of scores in order and indicate the number of times each score occurs. This would be a **frequency distribution table**. Where there is a large set of numbers, it is a more economical and meaningful way of representing the data. It also has the advantage that it can be represented pictorially in the form of a **histogram** or **frequency polygon** (see the next subsection).

As an illustration, if we take the raw data from the memory experiment as shown in Figure 3.1, we can organise it into a frequency distribution as follows:

● Arrange the scores in order from lowest to highest.
● Indicate how many times each score occurs (the frequency).

Figure 3.5 shows the data from Figure 3.1 reorganised in the form of a frequency distribution. It is helpful to indicate the number of scores at the foot of each column (N). N is also, of course, the sum of the frequencies.

FIGURE 3.4
Two examples of pie charts

(a) Number of males and
females scoring higher
than 10

(b) Proportion of total sales of
consumer durables

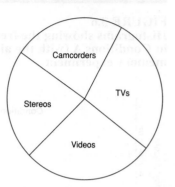

FIGURE 3.5
Frequency distribution table containing data from Figure 3.1

Frequency of scores (nonsense syllables correctly recalled).

Condition A (with the aid)		Condition B (without the aid)	
Score	Frequency	Score	Frequency
		5	1
		6	1
		7	1
		8	2
9	2	9	3
10	2	10	4
11	3	11	2
12	5	12	3
13	4	13	2
14	3	14	1
15	1		
	N = 20		N = 20

Note that this way of organising the data includes all the information given in the table of raw scores but more clearly and succinctly. By looking at Figure 3.5, we can get a much clearer picture of the relationship between the two sets of scores.

FIGURE 3.6
Histograms showing the frequency of scores of participants in Conditions A (with the aid) and B (without the aid) of the memory experiment

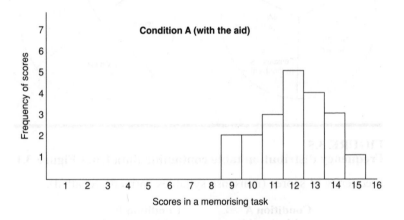

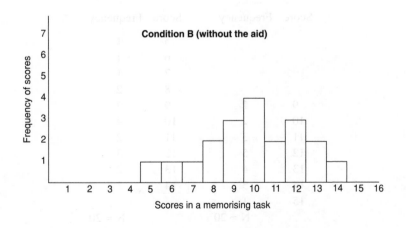

Histograms

A histogram is a graphical form of frequency distribution (see Figure 3.6). To convert the date from Figure 3.5 into two histograms, we would do the following:

- Draw vertical and horizontal axes.
- Mark the vertical axes with numbers to represent the frequency of the scores.
- Mark the horizontal axes in sections to represent the scores.
- Draw 'boxes' above each score to indicate the number of times it occurs.
- Ensure that all parts of the histograms are clearly labelled and that there is an overall title.

It is now possible to see at a glance that the scores in Condition A tend to be higher than those in Condition B. It is also obvious that the scores are more 'spread out' in Condition B. Note also that in a histogram, it is possible to spot the mode at a glance.

Grouped frequency distribution

In a study which generates a very wide range of frequencies from a large set of scores, it is usual to classify the data into classes or intervals, for example scores 1–5, 6–10, 11–15, and so on. This would then become a grouped frequency distribution. This can, of course, also be represented as a histogram.

Frequency polygons

Another way of pictorially representing the data from a frequency distribution would be in the form of a frequency polygon. Here the 'bars' of the histogram are repaced by dots and the height of each dot represents the frequency of occurrence of each score. This is illustrated in Figure 3.7, again using the data drawn from Figure 3.5.

Frequency polygons are especially useful where we want to compare two or more sets of data, since we can plot them on the same pair of axes.

FIGURE 3.7
Frequency polygon of the scores from Conditions A (with the aid) and B (without the aid) in the memory experiment

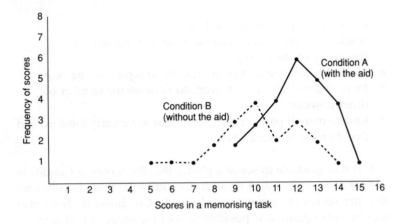

Normal distribution

The normal distribution (see also Chapter 1) is a special kind of frequency distribution which is often arrived at where a large set of measures is collected and then organised into a histogram. For example, suppose we recorded the IQ scores of 500 people randomly drawn from the population and then organised the scores into a frequency distribution; the resulting histogram would look something like the one in Figure 3.8. (Note that there are so many 'bars' that the end product appears as a smooth line.)

This is a very well-known 'bell-shaped' distribution, which often occurs where a large number of measurements are taken of naturally occurring phenomena, for example, people's heights, weights, foot sizes and many other things.

Figure 3.8
A normal distribution showing the frequency of IQ scores in a sample of 500 people

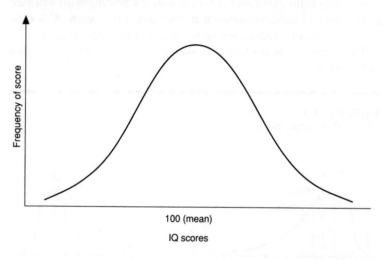

Characteristics of the normal distribution

- The mean, median and mode all occur at the same point (the highest point of the curve).
- It is symmetrical on either side of the central point of the horizontal axis – the pattern of scores is exactly the same above the mean as it is below.
- A large number of scores fall relatively close to the mean on either side. As the distance from the mean increases, the scores become fewer.

The normal curve of distribution can only occur when the data are continuous, that is, at interval or ratio level, rather than separate or discrete, as in frequency data.

Skewed distributions

Sometimes, a set of scores will yield a distribution that is skewed rather than normally distributed. (You may have found this in your own group experiments where you are dealing with a biased rather than a random sample of participants.) In a skewed distribution, the mean, median and mode will fall at different points.

There are two main kinds of skewed distribution, as indicated in Figure 3.9.

FIGURE 3.9
Skewed distributions

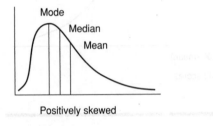

Positively skewed

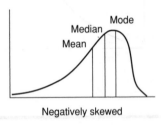

Negatively skewed

Notice the postion of the mean, median and mode in each distribution: the mode is obviously the highest point, where the majority of scores are; the mean is furthest away from the mode; and the median falls between the two.

In a **positive skew**, the mean is misleadingly high – 'pulled up' by a few extremely high scores; in a **negative skew**, the mean is relatively low – 'pulled down' by a few very low scores.

A skewed distribution often occurs when a small number of measurements are made or where the measurements are taken from a biased sample drawn from a normally distributed population. It might occur also in a distribution plotted from a set of scores drawn from a test which was very easy (too many high scores, therefore a negative skew) or very hard (too many low scores, therefore a positive skew).

Measures of dispersion

We have seen that the mean, median and mode are used to summarise sets of numbers by indicating a score which is representative of the set. However, this does not give all the information we need when describing and comparing sets of scores. In order to give a more complete picture, we need to know also how spread out – dispersed – the scores are.

There are a number of measures of dispersion, but we shall examine just three: the variation ratio, the range and the standard deviation.

The **variation ratio** is used in conjunction with the mode (the most frequently occurring value). It allows us to make a judgment about how representative a measure of central tendency the mode is for a particular set of numbers. We can do this by assessing what proportion of the numbers is not 'modal'. Consider the following set of numbers:

2, 4, 6, 7, 7, 7, 8, 8, 9, 10, 12   Mode = 7

Three numbers (7) are 'modal' and eight are not.

The variation ratio is found by calculating what proportion of the total scores the 'nonmodal' scores constitute. To do this, we divide eight (number of 'nonmodal' scores) by eleven (total number of scores):

$8 \div 11 = 0.727$

We can now state that 0.727 of our scores are not modal. This implies, of course, that 0.273 are modal. We could represent these figures as percentages by multiplying them by 100. In this case, we could then say that 72.7 per cent of the scores are not accounted for by the mode. This suggests that the mode is not very representative of this particular set of numbers.

The **range** indicates the difference between the lowest score and the highest, for example:

(a) 5 23 33 6 32 27   Mean = 21   Range = 28

(b) 21 19 22 18 25 21   Mean = 21   Range = 7

Note that the means of these two sets of scores are the same, but the dispersions, as indicated by the range, are very different.

As with the mean, the range only gives a good description if the scores are fairly bunched together. If there are one or two extreme scores, as in set (a) above, use of the range can be misleading.

A more powerful measure of dispersion, which reflects how spread out the scores are about the mean, is known as the **standard deviation**.

Standard deviation

The standard deviation indicates the average of the distances of all the scores around the mean. Box 3.3 shows one method of calculating it. The larger the standard deviation of a set of scores, the more spread out they are relative to the mean. Figure 3.10 illustrates two distributions, one with a large and one with a small standard deviation.

FIGURE 3.10
Histograms illustrating large and small standard deviations

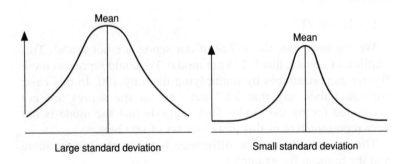

Large standard deviation   Small standard deviation

BOX 3.3   CALCULATING THE STANDARD DEVIATION (SD)

Example: Calculating the SD of the numbers 12, 10, 8, 4, 18, 8

1. First calculate the mean of the scores   **(10)**

2. Subtract the mean from the value of each score, ignoring the signs. This will give you the deviations   **(2, 0, 2, 6, 8, 2)**

3. Square each deviation   **(4, 0, 4, 36, 64, 4)**

4. Add together all the squared deviations. This will give you the sum of squares   **(112)**

5. Count the number of scores and subtract one   **(6 – 1 = 5)**

6. Divide the sum of squares in step 4 by the value in step 5. This is the variance   **(22.4)**

7. Take the square root of the variance found in Step 6. This is the standard deviation   **(4.73)**

Note: The formula for the standard deviation is $\dfrac{\Sigma(X - \overline{X})^2}{N}$

where   X = individual score
$\overline{X}$ = mean of scores
N = number of scores

However, where we are calculating the SD of a sample of scores in order to estimate the variability within the larger population, using the above formula gives a slight underestimation of the variability. Therefore, in practice, the following formula is usually used when dealing with a sample:

$$\frac{\Sigma(X - \overline{X})^2}{N - 1}$$

The standard deviation is expressed in terms of the scores you are analysing; for example, if a standardised IQ test were administered to the general population, it would usually yield a mean of 100 and a standard deviation of 15 (IQ points). It has useful mathematical properties that can be used in more complicated analyses. Many inferential statistical tests involve comparing the means and standard deviations of two or more sets of scores.

The standard deviation and the normal distribution

There is a very interesting and useful relationship between the standard deviation and the normal curve of distribution. If we have a set of scores which approximates to a normal distribution, a knowledge of the mean and standard deviation of the scores would enable us to draw the distribution.

FIGURE 3.11
The standard deviation and the normal distribution

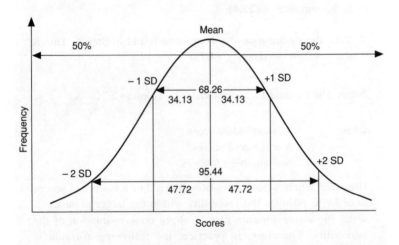

A very important property of the normal distribution is that it always has the same proportion of scores falling between particular points of the distribution. As illustrated in Figure 3.11,

68.26 per cent of all scores fall between one standard deviation below the mean (–1SD) and one standard deviation above the mean (+1SD); 95.44 per cent of all scores fall between two standard deviations below the mean (–2SD) and two standard deviations above the mean (+2SD). Also, because we know the normal curve of distribution is symmetrical, we know that 50 per cent of all the scores fall below the mean and 50 per cent above the mean.

FIGURE 3.12
Normal distribution showing the heights of the Martian population

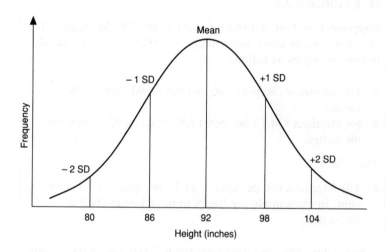

Let us examine how this can be helpful. Imagine that we know from population statistics that the mean height of the Martian population is 92 inches and that the standard deviation is 6 (inches). A normal distribution drawn from a random sample of heights in the Martian population would look like Figure 3.12.

Remember that the curve represents a histogram, so that there are numbers of scores (heights of Martian people) in any part of the distribution in proportion to the area occupied.

It follows from the information in Figure 3.12 that:

- 50 per cent of the Martian population would have heights below the mean and 50 per cent above;
- 68.26 per cent (34.13 per cent below the mean and 34.13 per cent above the mean) of the Martian population would have heights between 86 inches (−1SD) and 98 inches (+1SD); and
- 95.44 per cent (47.72 per cent below the mean and 47.72 per cent above the mean) of the Martian population would have heights between 80 inches and 104 inches.

■ EXERCISE 3.2

Suppose you take a random sample of 200 Martians. It is possible to calculate how many are likely to have heights below 98 inches as follows:

- 100 Martians (50 per cent) fall below 92 inches (the mean).
- 68 Martians (34.13 per cent) fall between 92 inches and 98 inches.

Therefore:

- 168 Martians (50 per cent + 34.13 per cent = 84.13 per cent) in our sample are likely to have heights below 98 inches.

  See if you can calculate how many Martians in the sample are likely to have heights below 86 inches. The answer is at the end of the section. Consult Figures 3.11 and 3.12 to check your calculations.

Now try the following exercises.

■ **EXERCISE 3.3**

A maths test is given to 200 children. The mean of the resulting scores is 60 and the standard deviation is 8. Draw the distribution using Figure 3.12 as a guide. See if you can calculate:

(a) how many children scored between 52 and 68;
(b) how many children scored below 52; and
(c) how many children scored above 68.

Note: You are being asked 'How many children?' not 'What proportion?'

The answers are on the next page.

z scores

z scores have already been described in Chapter 2, Section V.

It is possible to express any score as a number of standard deviations above or below the mean. For example, if you have a set of scores with a mean of 50 and a standard deviation of 10, the mean score (50) would be zero, one of 55 would be +0.5 and one of 45 would be –0.5 (One standard deviation is 10, therefore half a standard deviation [0.5] is 5). These are known as z scores. They are commonly employed where it is necessary to compare performances on a range of different tests. Because the tests are likely to have different means and standard deviations, it would not make sense to compare results directly, so they are converted to z scores. This can only be done, however, when the scores are normally distributed.

It is possible to work out the probability (p) of any particular z score occurring; a table of the probability of z scores is included at the end of this book (Appendix III, Table B). The figures in the table identify the proportions of scores falling between the mean and any z score.

Self-assessment questions

1. Briefly explain the purpose of descriptive statistics. Give two examples.
2. What is meant by 'measures of central tendency'? Explain which is the preferred one and in what circumstances it might be misleading to use it.
3. Briefly explain the terms 'frequency distribution', 'histogram' and 'frequency polygon'.
4. In what circumstances would you expect to obtain a normal distribution? What are its characteristics?
5. Draw a rough diagram of a negatively skewed distribution. In what circumstances would you expect it to occur?
6. Explain what is meant by 'standard deviation'. What is its relationship to a normal distribution?

■ ■ **ANSWERS TO EXERCISE 3.1**

(a) mean = 78   median = 78
    Since the two values are the same and the scores are fairly bunched together, one would use the mean as the preferred average.

(b) mean = 59   median = 77.5
    Because there are two very atypical scores, the mean of 59 is not exactly representative of the set. Therefore, it would make sense to use the median as a typical score.

■ ■ **ANSWER TO EXERCISE 3.2**

31 Martians are likely to have heights below 86 inches
(50 per cent − 34.13 per cent = 15.87 per cent)

■ ■ **ANSWERS TO EXERCISE 3.3**

(a)   136 children (68 per cent)
(b)   32 children (16 per cent)
(c)   32 children (16 per cent)

SECTION II STATISTICAL INFERENCE AND SIGNIFICANCE

Inferential statistics

In the last section, we dealt fully with a range of descriptive statistics, which you will recall are used to describe and summarise data. We also indicated that there is another category of statistics which is useful when analysing and drawing conclusions about the results of a study. These are known as **inferential statistics**. Before considering inferential statistics in detail, it is important to look again at the concept of population (see Chapter 1) in relation to statistical testing.

Populations and statistical tests

You will remember from the section on populations and samples in Chapter 1, that when carrying out research, the term 'population' refers to the entire parent group – of humans, animals or even things – from which a sample is selected for testing. It implies that we are dealing with a group that shares some common characteristic. Examples of populations are children under five years old, females living in England, people over six feet tall, sheep in Australia, sufferers from autism, dolphins in captivity, apples grown in Worcestershire, and so on. In statistics, the term 'population' relates to some kind of numerical aspect of the group in which we are interested. It might be IQ scores of people in England and Wales, heights of people living in Ireland or aggression ratings in children.

If we wished to carry out an experiment into, for example, two different ways of teaching mathematics to five-year-olds, we would not of course be able to test the whole population, but would test a sample drawn from the population (see Chapter 1). The sample would be split into two groups, each being taught by a different method, before being assessed. In assessing the results, we would be asking the question 'Is one set of numbers substantially different from the other?' If after applying an appropriate statistical test, we decide that the two sets of numbers are significantly different, we would then conclude that they had been drawn from *two different populations*. If on the other hand, we find no significant difference between the two sets of numbers, we would conclude that they were drawn from the *same* population. This is a very important idea in statistical testing. (The concept of significance will be discussed later.)

Probability

Inferential statistics make use of the concept of **probability** to determine the likelihood that the results – either a difference between two sets of scores or a correlation – might have occurred by chance.

Consider, for example, the data from our memory experiment described in Section I of this chapter. The results, as shown in the frequency distribution and histogram illustrated in Figures 3.5 and 3.6, indicate that there appears to be a difference between the number of nonsense syllables recalled by the experimental group and the number recalled by the control group. Overall, the experimental group appear to have recalled more syllables; the mean score for this group is certainly higher. Can we be sure, however, that this difference has been brought about by the independent variable – the memory aid – thus allowing us to accept the alternative hypothesis? It is possible that it has simply occurred by chance and that we are looking at two samples drawn from the same population. Applying a statistical test will help us to decide whether or not the difference is sufficient to give us the confidence to discount this chance. If we decide we do have the confidence, we would reject the null hypothesis and accept the alternative hypothesis. If after applying a statistical test, we decide that the probability of a chance result is small enough to be discounted, we would say that we had obtained a **significant** result. Before considering this term further, let us look a little more closely at the concept of **probability**.

As you may already know, probability is to do with how likely it is that a particular situation, event or pattern of numbers occurs by chance. This is something we consider quite often in everyday life. For example, how often have you heard the phrase 'There is a fifty/fifty chance that... (something will happen)' or 'There is a million to one chance of it happening'. Put another way, 'fifty/fifty' means that there is an equal chance of something happening or not happening; 'million to one' means that it is a million times more likely that one thing will happen rather than another.

There are three main ways of expressing probability:

- As a ratio.

1 in 100, 2 to 1, 1 in 20 (or 1:100, 2:1, 1:20) are examples.

- As a percentage.

100 per cent probability of something happening means that it is certain to happen.

0 per cent probability means that it is certain *not* to happen.

5 per cent probability means there is a 5 in 100 (or 1 in 20) chance that it will happen, and so on.

- As a decimal fraction between 0 and 1.

0   0.1   0.2   0.3   0.4   0.5   0.6   0.7   0.8   0.9   1

Certain not to happen   Definitely will happen

Note that a probability of 1 is the same as a probability of 100 per cent, so that a 5 in 100 probability may be expressed as follows:

5:100 or 5 per cent or 0.05. (This is usually written as $p = 0.05$.)

Thus:

0.5 probability ($p = 0.5$) means that the chance of something happening is 50 per cent, 1 in 2 or 50:50 (an example of this would be the probability of throwing a head or a tail if you tossed a normal coin);

$p = 0.1$ means that there is a 10 per cent or 1 in 10 probability;

$p = 0.05$ means that there is a 5 per cent or 1 in 20 probability;

$p = 0.01$ means that there is a 1 per cent or 1 in 100 probability.

When the results of experimental and other research work are analysed, the levels of probability most commonly employed are $p \leq 0.05$ or $p \leq 0.01$ (where $\leq$ means 'equal to or less than').

Figure 3.13 gives some examples of probabilities expressed as ratios, percentages and decimals.

FIGURE 3.13
Probabilities expressed as ratios, percentages and decimals

Event	Likelihood	Decimal	Percentage	Ratio
That you are alive!	Certain	1.00	100	100:100
A tossed coin coming up tails	One in two	0.5	50	50:100
That a dice will come up with a 4	One in six	0.16	$16^2/_3$	$16^2/_3$:100
(Used when analysing research results)	One in 20	0.05	5	5:100
	One in 100	0.01	1	1:100
That you will walk on Mars next week	Impossible	0.00	0	0:100

In analysing the results of studies, we are constantly asking the question 'What is the probability that this difference/relationship occurred by chance?' Statistical tests such as the Sign, Mann-Whitney and Wilcoxon tests and others described in the next chapter will allow us to estimate this probability. If the probability is small, we can have confidence that the difference (or relationship) is not due to chance. But what do we mean by 'small' – how small? By convention, researchers commonly decide upon 5 per cent or less probability ($p \leq 0.05$) as the point at which they will have enough confidence in their results to reject the null hypothesis. This is known as the 5 per cent **level of significance**. It indicates that there is an equal, or less than, 5 per cent probability that you are just observing two samples from the same population rather than from two different populations, one influenced by the independent variable and one not. In such a case, we would say that we had obtained a **significant** result.

Tests of significance

Level of significance, then, refers to the level of probability that the results obtained from a study are likely to have occurred by chance. After carrying out a study, we would prepare appropriate descriptive statistics and study them carefully. In some rare cases, this is sufficient to indicate that the results allow us to have confidence that the difference or relationship we were exploring actually exists. However, in the majority of cases, the results are not so clear cut, and it is necessary to apply an inferential statistical test known as a **test of significance** before we can be confident enough to reject the null hypothesis and decide to accept the alternative hypothesis (for example, that the independent variable has had a real effect on the dependent variable).

Two general kinds of tests of significance covered in this book are as follows:

- **tests of difference**, which, as the name suggests, enable you to test the significance of a difference between two or more sets of data (see Figure 3.18 for a summary and Chapter 4 for details of how to calculate some tests of difference);
- **tests of correlation**, which allow you to examine the degree of *relationship* between two variables (see Section III of this chapter for an explanation of the principles of correlational analyses and Chapter 4 for details of how to calculate two tests of correlation).

Let us explore how we might use one test of difference in a hypothetical experiment. Suppose Mrs Chancer, a primary school teacher, believes that playing a word game such as Scrabble will help children's spelling. She decides to test this by first giving a spelling test to all the children in her class.

Her experimental hypothesis is that after playing Scrabble daily for two weeks, spelling performance will be better.

The null hypothesis says that any difference observed will be the result purely of chance factors – spelling performance is not in fact improved.

After two weeks of playing Scrabble every day, Mrs Chancer gives the children another spelling test.

The results look like this:

Number of correct spellings

CHILD	TEST 1 (Before playing Scrabble)	TEST 2 (After playing Scrabble)
1	45	56
2	10	22
3	50	75
4	44	45
5	17	35
6	58	60
7	36	45
8	39	43
9	55	50
10	20	39
11	45	60
12	48	72
Mean	38.92	50.17

Do you think there is a difference in the two sets of scores? Has the Scrabble made a difference? The mean scores do indicate that there is a marked difference between the two sets of scores. One way of answering these questions would be to apply a test of significance. Accordingly, Mrs Chancer decides that a Sign test is appropriate. (This is described in detail in the next section.) She settles on a 5 per cent ($p \leq 0.05$) significance level as her level of confidence. The Sign test is one of a number of tests which will examine whether or not there is a significant difference between two sets of scores – remember that 'significant' in this context means 'unlikely to have occurred by chance'.

The stages Mrs Chancer goes through are these:

1. Formulates a null and an alternative hypothesis.
2. Decides upon an acceptable significance level.
3. Administers the two tests to the children.

4. Computes a Sign test in order to estimate the probability that the results occurred by chance.

    Look at Chapter 4, Section I and you will see the procedure for calculating a Sign test, along with the calculations for Mrs Chancer's 'Scrabble' experiment. The statistics arrived at are $X = 1$ and $N = 12$. Note that it is possible to assess whether or not this answer is significant by comparing it with the special table of critical values drawn up for the Sign test (see Appendix III, Table E). Each statistical test has its own table of critical values (probabilities, created by statisticians, of the null hypothesis being true under different circumstances). For the Sign test, our value must not exceed the table value for us to accept that a result is significant. (Note that for some other significance tests, our value must be *equal to* or *better than* the table value.) When Mrs Chancer consults the table of critical values, the figures tell her that she has a significant result at the 0.05 level. (The probability that the result occurred by chance is equal to or less than 1 in 20.)

5. On the basis of the Sign test result, she decides to reject the null hypothesis and to accept her experimental hypothesis that playing Scrabble for two weeks did improve children's spelling performance. She is able to say that playing Scrabble for two weeks *significantly* improved the children's spelling.

Although $p \le 0.05$ is the level of significance most commonly adopted by scientists, there may be occasions when you wish to choose a different level of significance. For example, if you wish to have even more confidence in your results you might adopt the more stringent $p \le 0.01$ level. Significance at this level tells us that there is a one in a hundred or less probability that the results occurred by chance. The level chosen would depend upon how crucial might be the correctness of our findings. For example, if we were carrying out research in which a significant result might overturn a well-established theory, we might wish to have the confidence of the $p \le 0.01$ level of significance or even the more stringent $p \le 0.001$ level (one in a thousand or less probability that the results occurred by chance) before we decided to accept our experimental hypothesis.

Figure 3.14 shows a summary of the procedure you should follow if you carry out an experiment and wish to calculate the significance of your findings.

FIGURE 3.14
Finding statistical significance

1. Formulate hypotheses and design study

2. Decide on an acceptable significance level (usually $p \leq 0.05$)

3. Collect data

4. Choose an appropriate statistical test (see Section III of this chapter)

5. Calculate the relevant statistic

6. Consult the table of critical values

7. Decide whether the result is significant and whether you will reject the null hypothesis and accept the alternative hypothesis

Whatever level of significance is chosen, it should be remembered that we are dealing with probabilities rather than certainties. This means that there may be occasions on which our conclusions are wrong – a result that was claimed to be significant was *not* due to the effect of the independent variable, or a nonsignificant result did in fact indicate a real effect of the independent on the dependent variable. Such mistakes are known respectively as **type 1** and **type 2** errors (see also Chapter 1, Section I).

Type I and type II errors

A type I error occurs when you reject the null hypothesis and accept the alternative hypothesis when in fact there was no real difference (or similarity). The observed difference was just the difference between two samples from a single population. This is most likely to occur when you have chosen a less stringent significance level such as $p \leq 0.05$. You have said that you will accept that there are indeed two different populations because the probability of this not being the case is equal to or less than five in a hundred.

A type II error is the converse of this. You have accepted the null hypothesis and concluded that there is no real effect observed when in fact there was a significant difference (or similarity). This will be more likely to occur if you adopt a very strict significance level, perhaps 1 per cent ($p \leq 0.01$). You have in effect said that you will not accept that your samples come from two different populations unless the probability is equal to or less than one in a hundred that they have come from just one population.

Which statistical test should I choose?

It is suggested that you refer to Figure 3.18 at the end of this chapter as you consider this question.

Which test you choose in order to analyse your data will depend upon two initial factors:

- Whether the data you have collected are independent or related. This will depend upon the kind of research design you are using: related measures, independent measures or matched pairs (see Chapter 2, Section II). Some tests, for example, the Sign test and Related t-test, are only suitable for use with related measures designs; others, for example Chi-squared (X^2) and Independent t-Test, are used only where you have an independent measures design. Note that a matched pairs design is treated as though it is a related measures design. (Note also that there are special tests, for example Spearman's rho (ρ) and Pearson's Product Moment, which deal with correlational analyses.) All these tests and some others are explained fully in the next chapter.
- The level of measurement of your data: nominal, ordinal, interval or ratio (see Introduction). These levels of measurement lead to two different kinds of statistical test. Nominal and ordinal lead to **non-parametric** tests, while with interval and ratio level data, **parametric** tests can be considered. Let us consider these two kinds of tests in turn.

Non-parametric tests. The main feature of these tests is that they work only on nominal or ranked (ordinal) data. Indeed, they were devised specifically to deal with data which do not have the sophisticated mathematical properties of interval or ratio data. Non-parametric tests are relatively free of restrictions in their use, in contrast to the more powerful and sophisticated parametric tests. Remember that you can always convert your interval or ratio scores to nominal or ordinal, but not the other way round.

Parametric tests. These tests work on the basis that a number of assumptions have been made about the nature of the data being analysed:

● The data analysed are at the interval or ratio level of measurement.
● The data from the two (or more) conditions are drawn from a population of scores which is normally distributed (see Section I). Parametric tests should not be used where it is obvious from the data collected that the distribution is skewed.
● The two (or more) sets of data being analysed are drawn from populations of scores which have similar variances (see Section I). This concept is referred to as **homogeneity of variance**.

As far as the first two assumptions are concerned, you may be thinking 'How will I know whether my data are suitable?' There is no simple answer to this question. It is also important to remember that it is the **population of scores** from which the sample is drawn that is at issue, rather than the scores themselves. However, the following guidelines may be followed in order to arrive at a decision.

1. To decide whether your scores indicate a normal distribution, there are two stages:

   ● You would first give them the 'eyeball test', that is, scrutinise them carefully in order to make an initial judgment about whether the population they are drawn from is normally distributed.

- You may then wish to make a more precise assessment by drawing up a frequency distribution of the scores (see Section I) or applying a Chi-squared test of 'goodness of fit' (see Chapter 4). This will allow you to make an assumption about the population from which the scores are drawn. In practice, at this stage in your statistical career, it is probably sufficient to examine the scores carefully and make a judgment.

2. To decide whether your sets of scores support the assumption of homogeneity of variance (see above) is relatively straightforward and again there are two stages:

- Give your data the 'eyeball test'. If there seems to be a similar amount of spread in each set, that may be sufficient.
- To be more precise, the variance, remember, is a measure of how 'spread out' the scores are and, as explained in Section I, it is directly related to the standard deviation (it is the standard deviation squared). Therefore, you might then compare the standard deviations of the sets of scores. If one set of scores has a very small standard deviation and the other a very large one, the criterion of homogeneity of variance is clearly very unlikely to have been met.

   But how similar do the variances of the sets of scores have to be? A technique known as an F test or variance–ratio test (see Appendix III, Table J) will show whether there is a significant difference in the sample variances. This will allow a judgment to be made about the population from which the scores are drawn. However, this may, again, in practice not be necessary. Examining the sets of scores and comparing their standard deviations should be sufficient.

To summarise, then, strictly, unless your data supports the three assumptions explained above, a parametric test should not be used; you should convert your data to ordinal or nominal form and use an appropriate non-parametric test. In practice, the last two assumptions (normality and homogeneity of variance) are sometimes ignored. This happens in particular with the two t-tests. They are said to be **robust** and will give a reasonably accurate result even where the parametric assumptions are not fully met.

The power of a test

Before leaving this discussion of parametric tests, here is a brief explanation of what is meant by 'more powerful', a term which is often used in connection with these tests. This means that the tests are more sensitive than non-parametric tests and are more likely to give an accurate assessment of significance for the following reason:

● Because the tests work on interval or ratio data, they have more information available to them than tests which make use only of nominal or ordinal data. They take account of the actual scores, rather than simply, say, the rank order of the scores. Therefore, a more confident decision can be made about whether to accept or reject the null hypothesis than can be made after using a non-parametric test.

Finally, a word of caution. Any test which is used on unsuitable data drawn from a poorly designed study is unlikely to give a satisfactory result. Using unsatisfactory data or the wrong statistical technique may lead to your accepting the experimental hypothesis falsely – a type I error – or failing to detect a real effect which is actually there – a type II error.

Self-assessment questions

1. Explain what is meant by 'inferential statistics'. Refer to the concepts of 'probability' and 'population'.
2. Express the following in words: $p \leq 0.05$; $p \leq 0.01$; $p \leq 0.10$.
3. What do you understand by 'significance level'? Outline the steps you would take if you carried out an experiment and then wished to assess the significance of your data.
4. What are the assumptions of a parametric test of significance?
5. Outline two factors that will influence your choice of a test which is suitable for analysing the results of an experiment.

SECTION II   CORRELATION

The use of the statistical technique of correlation has been discussed in Chapter 2, Section IV. It is recommended that you re-read that section before proceeding to examine correlation further.

Remember that correlation is a statistical technique which allows us to examine the degree of relationship between two variables. An example might be the relationship between the amount of violent TV viewed by a sample of primary school children and the level of aggression they display in the school playground. To investigate this, it would be necessary first to define (a) what should be categorised as 'violent TV', and (b) what behaviour exhibited by the children would be categorised as 'aggressive' and how each would be measured. It should then be possible to collect pairs of scores for each child and to carry out a correlational analysis.

Ways of expressing correlation

One way to express correlation is graphically, by means of a **scattergram**. Pairs of measurements (for example, 'violent TV' and 'aggression' as previously described) are plotted on a graph, and the pattern which the plots make indicates the relationship between the two measures. Additionally, **a correlation coefficient** can be worked out to express the relationship in figures. The maximum value of a correlation coefficient is 1, and it can be positive or negative; the minimum is 0. Chapter 4 contains a full explanation of the techniques involved in calculating a correlation coefficient.

In terms of interpreting scattergrams and correlation coefficients, it is helpful to note the following:

● If there is a **perfect positive correlation** between the two sets of measurements, the coefficient will be +1. For example, the number of gallons of petrol you put in your car will exactly match the cost in pounds. The more petrol you buy, the more it will cost. The scattergram will look something like this:

Gallons purchased	Cost in £
1	2
2	4
3	6
4	8
5	10
6	12
7	14

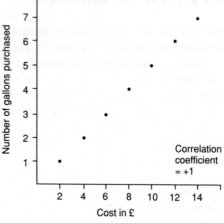

- If there is a **perfect negative relationship** between two sets of measurements, the correlation coefficient will be –1. (Note that –1 does *not* mean 'no relationship'.)

   Suppose you filled your car at the beginning of a journey and then at intervals along the way measured the amount of petrol left in the car as well as the distance you had travelled; there would be a perfect negative correlation. The more miles you have travelled, the less petrol you will have in the car. The scattergram would look something like this:

Miles travelled	Gallons left
20	5
40	4
60	3
80	2
100	1
120	0

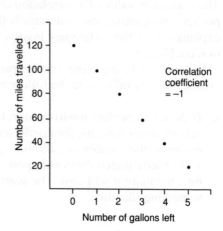

● Suppose that you wanted to test a hypothesis that there was a relationship between people's head circumference and their intelligence (as measured by a standard intelligence test); you would probably find that there was no relationship at all. The correlation coefficient would be zero, and a scattergram would show plots randomly scattered across the graph like this:

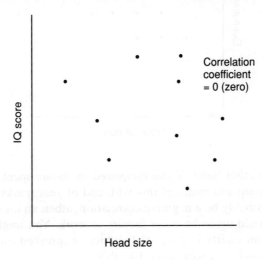

● In practice, in psychological research there are likely to be few perfect correlations, either positive or negative. Imperfect positive or negative correlations are expressed by decimal fractions. If you measured the number of hours devoted to study by a group of psychology students and matched this with the marks gained at the end of the year, you would probably get a positive correlation, but not a perfect one. There may be other factors likely to affect your results. You might get a correlation coefficient of, say, +0.6. A scattergram would look something like this:

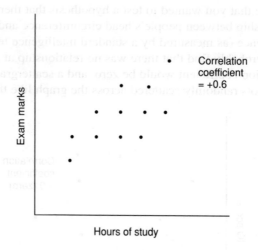

On the other hand, if you measured the hours spent in the pub by the group and matched this with end of year marks, the result would probably be a negative correlation, albeit an imperfect one. There would again be other factors at work. You might obtain a correlation coefficient of –0.4, which, expressed on a scatter-gram, would look something like this:

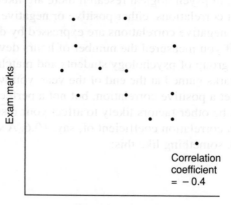

■ **EXERCISE 3.4**

Draw scattergrams for the following pairs of scores. What do the scattergrams tell you about the degree of relationship between variable A and variable B?

(a) Variables		(b) Variables		(c) Variables	
A	**B**	**A**	**B**	**A**	**B**
5	5	11	5	10	2
8	8	9	7	8	1
3	3	7	4	7	3
4	4	5	9	5	4
11	11	6	2	2	10
6	6	4	5	4	6
2	2	8	10	7	5
7	7	5	7	3	9

Answers at the end of the section.

When you use the technique of correlation, it is important that you always first draw up a scattergram from the data you have collected. This will allow you to examine the kind of relationship that has emerged and spot **nonlinear trends** (not following a straight line – see next page) before you calculate a correlation coefficient.

Correlation coefficients and significance

There are a number of tests which can be used to calculate a correlation coefficient. Two of these – Spearman's Rank Order correlation (which is non-parametric) and Pearson's Product Moment (which is parametric) – are described in Chapter 4. Remember that a correlation coefficient always varies between 0 and 1, and it can be positive or negative.

The correlation coefficient is considered to be a descriptive statistic, the size of which indicates the degree of relationship between two variables. However, it can also be tested for significance in the way that the statistic from a test of difference can. In correlation, what is being examined is the probability that the relationship (rather than the difference) between two variables, for example viewing TV violence and aggression in children, occurred by chance. If this probability is 0.05 or less, we have a significant correlation and can infer that there is a relationship between TV violence and aggression. Bear in mind, though, that we could *not* infer that viewing TV violence *caused* aggression. (See the problem of cause and effect in Chapter 2, Section III.)

Limitations of tests of correlation

There are a number of kinds of relationship which, may not be accurately detected by the Spearman's or Pearson's tests; these are outlined below:

● Suppose you obtained data which, when plotted on a scattergram, produced a pattern like one of those in Figure 3.15. These are nonlinear relationships (forming a curved rather than a straight line) and would be described as **curvilinear relationships.**

FIGURE 3.15
Curvilinear relationships
Not suitable for Pearson's Product Moment test.

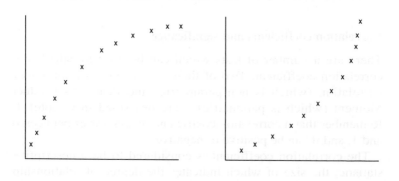

Spearman's rho (ρ) can be used without problems on scores which indicate curvilinear relationships, such as those in Figure 3.15. However, Pearson's test would not give a meaningful correlation coefficient and therefore should not be used.

● Another kind of curvilinear relationship which might be obtained can be seen in Figure 3.16. In both of these, the 'line' starts to change direction, resulting in an arched or U-shaped pattern.

FIGURE 3.16
Arched and U-shaped relationships

Not suitable for either Spearman's or Pearson's tests.

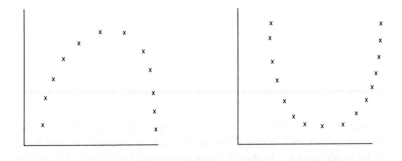

Where your scores produce an arched or U-shaped relationship, the data are too complex for either the Spearman's or the Pearson's test to deal with. Therefore, neither of these tests should be used.

● Another data pattern which needs to be treated with caution when calculating a correlation coefficient involves **outliers**. An outlier is a pair of scores which is extreme and not typical of the rest of the data. Figure 3.17 gives an example of a scattergram which indicates a fairly strong linear relationship apart from the position of one pair of scores – the outlier.

FIGURE 3.17
An outlier relative to a linear relationship

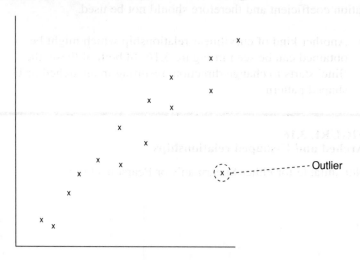

One or more outliers can have a very misleading effect on the interpretation of a correlation coefficient. A decision would have to be made about whether the outlier should be excluded from the analysis (you might be accused of misrepresenting your data) or included (you may fail to detect an otherwise strong relationship, therefore committing a type II error). One factor which may help you to decide is the size of your sample. With a large set of scores, an outlier would not exert as great an influence on the correlation coefficient as it would with a small sample. You might therefore decide to include it. However, if you do decide to exclude the outlier from your analysis, it is important that you state this clearly in your report.

Correlation and hypotheses

In a correlational study, the null hypothesis would predict that there is no relationship between the two variables under examination.

The alternative hypothesis could be either one-tailed or two-tailed (see Chapter 1). A one-tailed hypothesis would predict *either* that there would be a positive relationship *or* that there would be a negative relationship; a two-tailed hypothesis would predict that there was a relationship, but would not indicate *its direction*.

Self-assessment questions

1. What is the purpose of the statistical technique of correlation?
2. What is a scattergram? Why is it important to draw up a scattergram when you are assessing the degree of correlation between two sets of data?
3. Explain the term 'correlation coefficient'.
4. What do you understand by the 'problem of cause and effect'?
5. Explain how a one-tailed hypothesis might differ from a two-tailed hypothesis in a study which involved a correlational analysis.

■ ■ ANSWERS TO EXERCISE 3.4

Drawing scattergrams

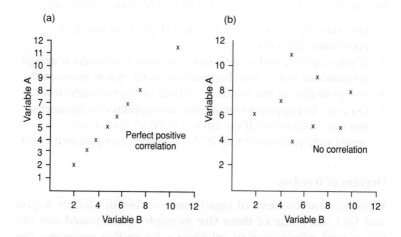

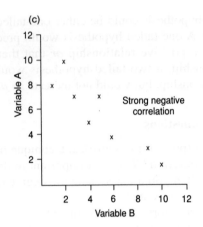

CHOOSING AN APPROPRIATE TEST

Now that you have completed Sections II and III, you are in a position to choose an appropriate test in order to analyse the data from an investigation. Ask yourself the following questions; the information in Figure 3.18 will help you to make a decision.

1. Do you require a test of difference (Part A) or a test of correlation (Part B)?
2. If you require a test of difference, is your experimental design repeated measures, matched pairs or independent measures?
3. Are your data at the nominal, ordinal or interval/ratio level?
4. Do your data appear to satisfy the assumptions of a parametric test (see Section II)? If the answer is 'Yes', choose an appropriate parametric test; if 'No', select a non-parametric test.

Degrees of freedom

When you use the tests of significance set out in Chapter 4, you will find that some of them (for example, Chi-squared and the two t-tests) require you to calculate a figure that represents the **degrees of freedom**. Degrees of freedom relate to the total number of values that have to be known, when the total is known, before any missing one can be filled in. An example may make this clearer.

Suppose you have £500, which you have decided to give to four different charities. Once you have decided on the amount you are giving to the first three charities – say £150, £150 and £100 – the amount you will give to the fourth charity – £100 – is fixed, given that the total sum you are donating is £500. In this example, there are four values; three of them are free to vary and the fourth is fixed. Therefore we would say that there were three degrees of freedom (3 df).

Here is another example. If I told you that the sum of six numbers was 25 and that five of the numbers were 3, 5, 2, 8 and 4, you would quickly deduce that the missing number was 3. In this case, there are five degrees of freedom (5 df) – five of the six numbers are free to vary.

In a statistical test, the degrees of freedom always relate to the number of scores or categories that are free to vary, given that the total number is known. You will find that when it is necessary to work out degrees of freedom, clear instructions are given.

FIGURE 3.18
Tests of significance

(A) TESTS OF DIFFERENCE

Kind of design	Type of data		
	NOMINAL	ORDINAL	INTERVAL/RATIO
Repeated measures	Sign test	Wilcoxon Signed Ranks	Related t-test
Matched pairs	Sign test	Wilcoxon Signed Ranks	Related t-test
Independent measures	Chi-squared (χ^2)	Mann-Whitney U test	Independent t-test

NON-PARAMETRIC   PARAMETRIC

(B) TESTS OF CORRELATION

	NOMINAL	ORDINAL	INTERVAL/RATIO
	No test, but χ^2 can be used (although it is a test of association)	Spearman's rho (ρ)	Pearson's Product Moment

NON-PARAMETRIC   PARAMETRIC

I could murder an Independent Tea Test !

Statistical Tests 4

It is intended that this chapter will enable you to:

1. understand how to calculate a number of inferential statistical tests, and
2. apply them to appropriate data drawn from your own investigations.

SECTION I   NON-PARAMETRIC TESTS

Remember that non-parametric tests work on nominal or ordinal data.

The Sign test

The Sign test can be used on data of nominal level or above.
It uses pairs of scores from a repeated measures (or matched pairs) design.

Rationale: It compares the number of differences between two conditions which are in one direction with the number in the other direction. This is assessed against what might be expected to occur by chance if the null hypothesis were true. In the table below, an improvement is indicated by a + sign and no improvement by a − sign.

Data from hypothetical study

Mrs Chancer, a primary school teacher, hypothesises that playing Scrabble will help children's spelling. After first giving the children a spelling test, she organises them to play Scrabble every day for two weeks. She then gives the children another spelling test to see if there is an improvement.

FIGURE 4.1
Data for Sign test: number of correct spellings before and after playing Scrabble

Participant number	Test 1	Test 2	Sign of difference
1	45	56	+
2	10	22	+
3	50	75	+
4	44	45	+
5	17	35	+
6	58	60	+
7	36	45	+
8	39	43	+
9	55	50	−
10	20	39	+
11	45	60	+
12	48	72	+

Procedure

1. Inspect the difference between each pair of scores. After disregarding pairs of scores which do not differ from each other, count the number of pairs of scores. This number is N.

Calculations on the above data

N = 12

2. Where the score in condition A is the larger, put a plus (+) sign in the last column. Where the score in condition B is the larger, put a minus (−) sign in the last column.

See 'Sign of difference' column.

3. Count the number of times the less frequent sign occurs. Call this X.

The least frequent sign is '−'. Therefore X = 1.

4. Consult the table of critical values (Appendix III, Table E). The values given relate to a two-tailed test. For a one-tailed test, the significance levels should be halved.

Since Mrs Chancer's hypothesis predicted that children's spelling would *improve*, we shall use a one-tailed test. Note that for a one-tailed test, significance levels are halved.

5. Find the relevant line of critical values relative to the value of N.

Consult the horizontal line next to N = 12.

6. Compare the value of X with the critical values. Since X must be equal to or less than the table value, find the highest level of significance for which X is still the same or smaller.

Our value of X is 1. The critical value for 'p ≤ 0.05' is 2, so we know the result is significant. However, the critical value for 'p ≤ 0.025' is 2 and the critical values under 'p ≤ 0.01 and 0.005' are both 1. Our value of X still does not exceed this. Therefore, we shall take the critical value for the lowest significance level of 0.005 as our result.

7. Make a statement of significance and decide whether or not to reject the null hypothesis in favour of the alternative hypothesis.

Our difference in results is significant at 0.005, p ≤ 0.005 (one-tailed). Therefore we shall accept the alternative hypothesis and conclude that playing Scrabble did improve the children's spelling.

Note that unless we used a representative sample of primary schoolchildren, we could not generalise our findings to the whole population of primary schoolchildren.

The Wilcoxon Signed Ranks test

This is used only on data of at least ordinal level. It uses pairs of scores from a repeated measures (or matched pairs) design.

Rationale: Like the Sign test, it examines the direction of differences between participants' scores in each condition. However, it is more sensitive since it also takes account of the relative size of the differences by examining their rank order. If the null hypothesis were true, we would expect the ranks to be randomly distributed between the two conditions. However, if the majority of lower ranks were in one condition, we would suspect that the alternative hypothesis were true, that there was a real difference between the two conditions.

Data from hypothetical study

A group of students were tested to discover how taken in they were by the Müller-Lyer illusion. The researchers hypothesised that there would be a difference between their performance in Condition A, where the Müller-Lyer figure was placed vertically, and Condition B, where the Müller-Lyer figure was placed horizontally.

FIGURE 4.2
Data for Wilcoxon Signed Ranks test: perception of the Müller-Lyer illusion in horizontal and vertical positions

1 Student	2 Con. A (Horizontal) mm	3 Con. B (Vertical) mm	4 Difference (A − B) mm	5 Rank of difference
1	15	17	−2	3.5
2	20	16	4	6.5
3	8	14	6	9
4	12	14	−2	3.5
5	23	16	7	10
6	11	19	−8	11
7	13	16	3	5
8	5	5	0	−
9	7	6	1	1.5
10	9	5	4	6.5
11	14	9	5	8
12	7	8	−1	1.5

Procedure	Calculations on the above data
1. Ignore the scores of any student who scored the same in both conditions.	Omit the results for student 8.
2. Calculate the difference between each score in Condition A and its equivalent in Condition B. Remember to subtract in the same direction each time.	See column 4 in Figure 4.2 (A–B).
3. Rank the differences, ignoring the sign of the difference. (This converts the data to ordinal level.) Give the smallest difference a rank of 1. (See Box 3.2 if you need help with ranking.)	See column 5 of Figure 4.2.
4. Add together the ranks for the least frequent sign. Call this value T.	The minus sign is the least frequent so add together the ranks for students 1, 4, 6 and 12, i.e. 3.5 + 3.5 + 11 + 1.5. This gives a value of T = 19.5.
5. Consult the table of critical values (Appendix III, Table F). Decide whether to take account of one- or two-tailed values.	Since there was no prediction of the *direction* of difference between Condition A and Condition B, only that there would *be* a difference, take account of two-tailed values.
6. Find the relevant line relative to the value of N. N is the number of pairs of scores after ignoring those with zero difference.	The relevant line is N = 11 (number 8 was discarded).
7. Find the lowest critical value which T does not exceed. If T is larger than all critical values, the result is not significant.	T is 19.5 and it is larger than all the table values. Therefore it is not significant.
8. Make a statement of significance and decide whether or not to reject the null hypothesis.	Since our result is not significant, we must retain the null hypothesis and reject the alternative hypothesis. We must conclude that the orientation of the Müller-Lyer illusion has no effect on students' perception of it.

Mann-Whitney U test

This works only on data of at least ordinal level.
It uses pairs of scores from an independent measures design.

Rationale: The test works on ranked data and compares the relative size of the scores in one condition with those in the other condition. Under the null hypothesis, we would expect to find the scores randomly distributed between the two conditions. If, however, most of the scores in one condition were higher in rank than most of the scores from the other condition, it would seem likely that we would find a real difference between the two sets of scores; that would imply that they were drawn from two different populations.

Data from a hypothetical study

A researcher sets out to compare the number of truancies occurring in two schools. Local concern had been expressed about one of them in particular. It was hypothesised that there would be a difference between the two schools in terms of the number of truancies. The data collected is the number of truancies occurring in the two schools over a 12-week period.

FIGURE 4.3
Data for Mann-Whitney U test: number of incidents of truancy occurring in two schools

1	2	3	4
Robin School	Ranks	Wren School	Ranks
10	12	6	2.5
9	10	11	15
12	17	8	8
14	19	7	5
15	20	8	8
17	22	11	15
16	21	7	5
13	18	5	1
10	12	8	8
11	15	6	2.5
		7	5
		10	12

Note that Robin School did not keep records for the last two weeks. Since this is an independent measures design, it is not necessary to have the same number of scores in each condition.

Procedure	Calculations/comments on the above data

Procedure

1. Rank all the scores as if they are one group. Give the smallest score a rank of 1. (See Box 3.2 for help with ranking.)

2. Add up all the ranks for the smaller group. (If the groups are the same, use either one.) Call this R.

3. Calculate U_1 and U_2 from the following formula, where

   R = Total of ranks in smaller group

   N_S = Number of scores in smaller group

   N_L = Number of scores in larger group

   $$U_1 = N_S N_L + \frac{N_S(N_S + 1)}{2} - R$$

   $$U_2 = N_S N_L - U_1$$

   (See Chapter 6 for help with tackling a formula.)

4. Choose the smaller of U_1 and U_2 and call it U.

5. Consult table of critical values (Appendix III, Table G) and decide whether to take account of one- or two-tailed values (on the basis of your hypothesis).

Calculations/comments on the above data

See columns 2 and 4 in Figure 4.3.

Robin School has the smaller number of scores.
Therefore, R = 166.

$$U_1 = 10 \times 12 + \frac{10(10 + 1)}{2} - 166$$

$$= 120 + \frac{110}{2} - 166$$

$$= 120 + 55 - 166$$

$$= 9$$

$$U_2 = (10 \times 12) - 9$$

$$= 120 - 9$$

$$= 111$$

$$U = 9$$

The prediction was that there would be a difference in incidents of truancy between Robin School and Wren School. There was no prediction about the *direction* of the difference.

7. Where your two values of N_S (smaller group) and N_L (larger group) meet, you will find the critical value which must not be exceeded for a two-tailed test. If you have previously decided on a significance level of 0.05, check the table value at this level first; then if your value of U is less, check the table value for 0.01 to see if U is still smaller.

8. Make a statement of significance and decide whether or not to reject the null hypothesis in favour of the alternative hypothesis.

Therefore, take account of two-tailed values.

$N_S = 10$ and N_L is 12.

The point at which these two meet shows a critical value of 29. Our value of U is 9, which is smaller than this, so we know it is significant at the 0.05 level. Look at the value shown at the 0.01 level. Here the table value is 21. Our value of $U = 9$ is still smaller, so it is significant at $p \leq 0.01$.

Our result is significant at 1 per cent, $p \leq 0.01$ (one-tailed). Therefore we shall accept the alternative hypothesis that there is a difference between the two schools. Robin School has a significantly larger number of truancies than Wren School.

Chi-squared (χ^2) test of association

This works on nominal (frequency) data.

It uses frequency data drawn from an independent measures design.

Note: Strictly speaking, the expected frequency in any cell should not fall below 5.

Rationale: χ^2 differs from the other tests considered in that it does not work on individual scores but on frequencies – the number of times an event occurs. (These are nominal data; see Chapter 3, Introduction.) For example, the number of absentees each day for a week in a school, goals scored in the Premier League last season, passes in the Psychology 'A' level examination this year.

What the test does is to examine the frequencies observed in a study, for example the number of people in different occupations who vote for various political parties, and compares these to the proportions in each category which might be expected to occur by chance. The research hypothesis might predict that people in some occupations would be more likely to vote Conservative and others more likely to vote Labour or Liberal Democrat; the null hypothesis would state that there would be no difference between the different occupational groups. The expected frequency represents what would be expected to occur under the null hypothesis.

Data from a hypothetical study

The 'A' level psychology results in two colleges produced the following distributions of A, B and C grades. The null hypothesis states that there is no difference between the colleges in terms of the proportions of students obtaining the different grades.

FIGURE 4.4
Data for Chi-squared (X^2) test: psychology 'A' level grades in two colleges

	A	B	C	Row totals
College X	6 (a)	42 (b)	15 (c)	63
College Y	8 (d)	42 (e)	46 (f)	96
Column totals	14	84	61	159 **Grand total**

Procedure

1. Draw up a table such as the one above. The raw data in the table is known as the observed frequency (F_o).

   Each 'box', known as a cell, is given a letter, (a) (b), and so on, so that it can be easily identified.

2. Obtain row totals, column totals and a grand total.

3. Calculate an expected frequency (F_e) for each cell by calculating as follows:

   $$\frac{\text{Row total} \times \text{column total}}{\text{grand total}}$$

   The expected frequencies relate to the proportions of passes expected to appear for each grade if there were no difference between the two colleges except that which might be expected due to chance factors.

Calculations on the data in Figure 4.4

1. Place the data in a box table and give each cell a letter (a), (b), (c), (d), (e), or (f) to identify it.

2. Insert row totals, column totals and a grand total.

3. Calculate the expected frequency (F_e) for each cell as follows:

   Cell (a) $F_e = \dfrac{63 \times 14}{159} = 5.55$

   Cell (b) $F_e = \dfrac{63 \times 84}{159} = 33.28$

   Cell (c) $F_e = \dfrac{63 \times 61}{159} = 24.17$

   Cell (d) $F_e = \dfrac{96 \times 14}{159} = 8.45$

   Cell (e) $F_e = \dfrac{96 \times 84}{159} = 50.72$

   Cell (f) $F_e = \dfrac{96 \times 61}{159} = 36.83$

4. Work out degrees of freedom by calculating (number of rows − 1) multiplied by (number of columns − 1). (In a simple, 2 × 2, Chi-squared test, the degrees of freedom are of course always 1.)

5. The formula for Chi-squared is as follows:

$$\chi^2 = \sum \frac{(F_o - F_e)^2}{F_e}$$

Note that $(F_o - F_e)$ means deduct the smaller frequency from the larger frequency, ignoring positive or negative signs.

Note also that some statisticians suggest that in a simple, 2 × 2 Chi-Squared test, a small adjustment known as the Yates Correction be applied. This involves subtracting 0.5 from the top line of the formula $(F_o - F_e)$, before it is squared.

Apply the formula to each cell in the table separately. The most straightforward way of doing this is by using a table such as the one below:

4. Work out the degrees of freedom (df)

$$df = (2 - 1) \times (3 - 1) = 2$$

5. Apply the formula for Chi-squared (χ^2)

See calculations below.

Cell	F_o	F_e	$(F_o - F_e)$	$(F_o - F_e)^2$	$\dfrac{(F_o - F_e)^2}{F_e}$
(a)	6	5.55	0.45	0.20	0.04
(b)	42	33.28	8.72	76.04	2.28
(c)	15	24.17	−9.17	84.09	3.48
(d)	8	8.45	−0.45	0.20	0.02
(e)	42	50.72	−8.72	76.04	1.50
(f)	46	36.83	9.17	84.08	2.28
					9.60

Total the numbers in the final column to arrive at the value of Chi-squared (X^2).

6. Consult the table of critical values for Chi-squared (Appendix III, Table D). Use the df and calculated Chi-squared (X^2) values to find the critical value.

6. Since no prediction was made that one college would have better results than the other, use values for a two-tailed test.

   Look at the line by 2 df. Our X^2 value of 9.60 is higher than the critical values for 0.05, 0.02 and 0.01. However, it is lower than the critical value at the 0.001 level. Therefore our result is significant at 0.01.

7. Make a statement of significance. Decide whether to accept or reject the null hypothesis.

   Take the highest table value which is lower than the calculated value of Chi-squared. If Chi-squared is lower than all the critical values, it is not significant. We must accept the null hypothesis since there is no significant difference between the frequencies.

7. Our result is significant at 1 per cent $p \leq 0.01$, 2 df (two-tailed). Therefore we shall reject the null hypothesis and conclude that there is a significant association between 'A' level grades and college. The difference between the colleges is unlikely to have occurred by chance.

   Note that when interpreting the results of a X^2 analysis, only a very careful inspection of the original data will tell us where the most substantial discrepancies lie. Looking at the data in Figure 4.4, College X had higher proportions of A and B grade passes than did College Y, while College Y had a higher proportion of C grade passes.

   Note also that the X^2 result alone cannot allow us to say that one college is 'better' than the other. There may be other factors responsible for the variation in grades between the two. For example, College X might have a higher proportion of mature, highly motivated students.

■ **EXERCISE 4.1**

Use the χ^2 table to check the significance of the following χ^2 values (all two-tailed). What is the probability that each value was due to chance factors?

(a) $\chi^2 = 2.95$; df = 1
(b) $\chi^2 = 16.54$; df = 8
(c) $\chi^2 = 32.61$; df = 12
(d) $\chi^2 = 4.24$; df = 3

Answers at end of section.

χ^2 test of 'goodness of fit'

A special use of χ^2 involves comparing data drawn from just one variable to see how far it matches a particular theoretical distribution. In such a case, it is known as χ^2 test of 'goodness of fit'. For example, suppose we wished to investigate the music preferences among members of a local youth club to find out whether there is a bias towards certain types of music. Each member is given just one choice.

Sample data

	Music preferences among youth club members					
	Classical	**Rock**	**Pop**	**Dance**	**Folk**	**Total**
Number of times each style was chosen	12	32	32	23	21	120

Calculation of χ^2 goodness of fit'

1. List the frequency of preferences for each type of music, as above. Total.

2. The expected number of choices for each kind of music if there were no real preference can be worked out as follows:

$$F_e = \frac{\text{Total number of observations}}{\text{Number of styles of music}}$$

$$= \frac{120}{5}$$

$$= 24$$

That is, 24 members would choose each style of music.

3. Calculate the degrees of freedom (df), where
   df = number of alternatives − 1
   = 5 − 1
   = 4

4. Apply the following formula for χ^2:

$$\chi^2 = \sum \frac{(F_o - F_e)^2}{F_e}$$

Calculations appear in the following table:

Style of music	F_o	F_e	$(F_o - F_e)$	$(F_o - F_e)^2$	$\frac{(F_o - F_e)^2}{F_e}$
Classical	12	24	12	144	6
Rock	32	24	8	64	2.67
Pop	32	24	8	64	2.67
Dance	23	24	1	1	0.04
Folk	21	24	3	9	0.38
					$\chi^2 = 11.75$

Consult the table of critical values for χ^2 (Appendix III, Table D) using the values for a two-tailed test.

With a df value of 4, the highest critical value that our value of χ^2 exceeds is 9.49. Therefore the result is significant at the 0.05 level. We can conclude that the distribution does not fit the distribution expected by chance. Rock and pop music are significantly preferred among the youth club members.

Chi-squared 'goodness of fit' and the normal distribution

When we discussed the assumptions for parametric tests (Chapter 3, Section II), we said that the data for both samples should approximate to a normal distribution. A normal distribution, you will remember, assumes that there is a fixed proportion of scores between the mean and one, two and three standard deviations from the mean. For example, 34.13 per cent of all the scores fall between the mean and one standard deviation above it.

Chi-squared 'goodness of fit' can be used to decide how closely a large sample approximates to a normal distribution. The one sample χ^2 can be used to test whether a set of scores is normally distributed. The table of z scores set out in Appendix III, Table B shows the proportion of scores which fall within various points on the distribution.

Spearman's rho (ρ) test of correlation

Spearman's rho (ρ) test can be used on related pairs of data at ordinal level or above.

Rationale: It is a test of correlation which describes the relationship (*not* the difference) between two variables.

Formula for Spearman's rho $\quad r_S = 1 - \dfrac{6\left(\Sigma d^2\right)}{N\left(N^2 - 1\right)}$

where d is the difference between pairs of ranks. N is the number of pairs.

Data from a hypothetical study

The following data give the scores of a group of students on a standard IQ test and on a measure of cognitive style (CS). It is hypothesised that there will be a correlation between the two sets of scores (two-tailed, since no prediction is made as to whether the relationship will be positive or negative).

FIGURE 4.5
Data for Spearman's rho test: scores from an IQ test and a test of cognitive style

1	2	3	4	5	6	7
Participant	IQ	CS	IQ rank	CS rank	Difference (d)	d^2
1	100	96	2	10	8	64
2	110	75	4	1	3	9
3	95	93	1	9	8	64
4	105	90	3	8	5	25
5	120	85	7	5	2	4
6	125	80	9	3	6	36
7	118	84	6	4	2	4
8	130	78	10	2	8	64
9	115	86	5	6	1	1
10	123	89	8	7	1	1
						$\Sigma d^2 = 272$

Procedure

1. Rank the scores on variable X (IQ) taking the lowest as 1.

2. Rank the scores on variable Y (CS) as before.

3. Subtract rank Y from rank X for each participant. (There is no need to indicate whether the difference is positive or negative.)

4. Square each difference.

5. Add up the d^2 scores.

6. Insert Σd^2 into the following formula:

$$r_S = 1 - \frac{6(\Sigma d^2)}{N(N^2 - 1)}$$

where N = number of pairs of scores.

7. Consult the table of critical values for Spearman's rho (Appendix III, Table H).

8. Find the relevant line relative to the value of N.

9. Find the lowest critical value that r_S exceeds.

10. Make a statement of significance and decide whether or not to reject the null hypothesis.

Calculations on the above data

See column 4.

See column 5.

See column 6 – difference between ranks.

See column 7 – squared difference scores (d^2).

Total of column 7 = 272 (Σd^2).

$$1 - \frac{6 \times 272}{10(10^2 - 1)}$$

$$= 1 - \frac{1632}{990}$$

$$r_S = -0.648$$

Take account of levels of significance for a two-tailed test. (In line with the hypothesis.)

The value of N is 10.

$r_S = -0.648$, which is equivalent to the table value at 0.05. Therefore it is significant at this level.

Since the result is significant, we decide to reject the null hypothesis and accept the alternative hypothesis. There is a significant *negative* correlation between IQ and cognitive style as measured by these particular tests. (This means that a high IQ score tends to be matched with a low CS score.)

■ ■ ANSWERS TO EXERCISE 4.1
(a) $p \leq 0.01$ (10 per cent)
(b) $p \leq 0.05$ (5 per cent)
(c) $p \leq 0.01$ (1 per cent)
(d) Greater than 0.1 (10 per cent)

SECTION II PARAMETRIC TESTS

A parametric test rests upon three assumptions (see Chapter 3, Section II):

● that there are interval or ratio scores;
● that there is **homogeneity of variance**. That is to say, the spread of the scores needs to be approximately similar. Variance has been discussed in Chapter 3, Sections I and II; and
● that the distribution of both populations is approximately 'normal'. Normal distributions have been discussed in Chapter 3, Section I.

Student's t-test

Rationale: The rationale for the t-tests for both related and independent samples involves the concept of the **standard error of the means** of the two samples being tested. This rests on the idea that if you were to take a number of random samples from a population, there would be some variation between them. The spread of these variations can be measured statistically in much the same way that the standard deviation from the mean is measured. Theoretically, the difference between the means of two random samples will be zero, not allowing for random variation. What the t-tests do is to test whether the difference in means observed is greater than that which might be accounted for by random variation. The t-ratio is defined as the observed difference minus the expected difference (zero), divided by the standard error of the difference between the means.

There are two t-tests in use, one for repeated measures and the other for independent measures.

Related t-test

The formula for the t-test for repeated (related) measures is as follows:

$$t = \frac{\sum D}{\sqrt{\dfrac{N.\sum(D^2) - (\sum D)^2}{N-1}}} \qquad \text{df } N-1$$

where D is the difference between pairs of scores and N is the number of pairs of scores.

There are several terms used to describe the kind of data for which this test is appropriate. These include:

- t-test for related samples;
- t-test for repeated samples (that is, where the same sample is tested under two conditions);
- t-test for paired samples; and
- t-test for matched samples.

The important point is that the data are paired; this could be done by testing the same sample of participants under different conditions and pairing the data obtained from each participant under one condition with that obtained under the other. Or it might be that the samples are 'matched' (see Chapter 2, Section II) for characteristics considered important to the study.

Example

In the card sorting task similar to that described in Chapter 6, participants have been asked to sort a pack of playing cards into two piles (black and red) and again into suits (hearts, diamonds, clubs and spades). The time taken (in seconds) to sort the cards for each procedure is taken and a t-test is used to determine whether the difference in time taken is significant. The prediction is that it will take longer where there are four choices (for suits) than for two (colours). Here are the results.

FIGURE 4.6
Data for a related t-test: a comparison of the time taken to sort cards into two and into four piles

Participant	Colours	Suits	Difference (D)	D^2
		Time taken to sort cards into two or four piles (in seconds)		
A	64	68	+4	16
B	82	96	+14	196
C	59	57	+2	4
D	82	75	−7	49
E	74	65	−9	81
F	90	95	+5	25
G	65	65	0	0
H	71	78	+7	49
I	87	80	−7	49
J	75	75	0	0
N=10			$\Sigma D = +9$	$\Sigma D^2 = 469$

A t-test for paired samples is carried out on the above results to determine whether there is any significant difference in the time taken to sort into two and to four piles; because the prediction is that it will take longer to sort into four piles, this is a one-tailed hypothesis. It is decided to reject the null hypothesis if the probability of a chance result is equal to or less than 5 per cent ($p \leq 0.05$). The stages of the test are as follows:

Procedure	Calculations on the above data
Stage 1: Find ΣD by totalling positive and negative differences separately and subtracting negatives from positives.	$+ 4 + 14 + 2 + 5 + 7 = 32 - 7 - 7 - 9$ $= 23 : \Sigma D = 9$

Note: As this is a one-tailed hypothesis, if ΣD had been negative, you would have had to retain the null hypothesis at Stage 1 as the results were in the opposite direction from that predicted.

Stage 2: Find the sum of the squared differences (ΣD^2). The easiest way to do this is to form a parallel column as above. Then multiply by N.	$469 \times 10 = 4690$
Stage 3: Square the sum of the differences $(\Sigma D)^2$.	$9^2 = 81$
Stage 4: Subtract the result of stage 3 from the result of stage 2.	$4690 - 81 = 4609$
Stage 5: Find $N - 1$.	$10 - 1 = 9$
Stage 6: Divide the result of stage 4 by the result of stage 5.	4609 divided by $9 = 512.11$
Stage 7: Find the square root of the result of stage 6.	$\sqrt{512.11} = 22.62$
Stage 8: Divide the result of stage 1 by the result of stage 7 to find t. t = 0.39, degrees of freedom 9 (N – 1).	9 divided by $22.62 = 0.39 = t$
Consult Appendix III, Table C to find the critical value of t at the $p \leq 0.05$ level (one-tailed) for 9 degrees of freedom.	Critical value is 1.83. As the value of t is less than this critical value, we can conclude that there is not a significant difference: it does not take significantly longer to sort cards into four piles than into two.

Note: If a two-tailed hypothesis had been decided upon (that is, that there was a difference in the time taken without predicting the direction of that difference), then the critical value of t would have been 2.26. The difference still would not have been significant.

The t-test for independent (unrelated) samples

Where the samples are independent and cannot be paired, a t-test for independent samples is used. Bear in mind the assumptions for parametric tests. A useful strategy in this, as in other parametric tests such as Pearson's Product Moment correlation, is to start by listing the scores in columns and alongside them their squares (that is, the scores multiplied by themselves). Then write down the sum of each column and the number of scores in each group. The formula for an unrelated t-test is as follows:

$$t = \frac{\overline{X}_A - \overline{X}_B}{\sqrt{\frac{\left\{\Sigma X_A^2 - \frac{(\Sigma X_A)^2}{n_A}\right\} + \left\{\Sigma X_B^2 - \frac{(\Sigma X_B)^2}{n_B}\right\}}{N-2} \times \frac{N}{n_A.n_B}}} \qquad \text{df } N-2$$

where $\overline{X}_A$ is the mean for sample A, $\overline{X}_B$ is the mean for sample B, n_A is the number of scores in sample A and n_B is the number of scores in sample B. X represents scores in either group. N represents the total number of scores.

Example

We can use a similar example. In a similar card sorting task, one group of participants (group A) was asked to sort into two piles (black and red), the other group (group B) was asked to sort into four piles (hearts, diamonds, clubs and spades). The hypothesis (two-tailed) was that there would be a difference in the time taken to sort into two and into four piles.

FIGURE 4.7
Data for an independent t-test: a comparison of times taken to sort cards into two and into four piles

The times in seconds taken by each group were as follows:

Group A (two piles)	Scores squared (X^2_A)	Group B (four piles)	Scores squared (X^2_B)
65	4225	68	4624
59	3481	60	3600
76	5776	65	4225
84	7056	75	5625
50	2500	78	6084
54	2916	57	3249
62	3844	54	2916
56	3136	96	9216
55	3025	70	4900
65	4225		
$n_A = 10$		$n_B = 9$	
$\overline{X}_A = 62.6$	$\Sigma X^2_A = 40184$	$\overline{X}_B = 69.2$	$\Sigma X^2_B = 44439$
$\Sigma X_A = 626$		$\Sigma X_B = 623$	

Procedure	Calculations on the above data
Stage 1: Subtract the smaller mean ($\overline{X}_A$) from the larger mean ($\overline{X}_B$).	$69.2 - 62.6 = 6.6$
Stage 2: In the first bracket, square ΣX_A and divide by n_A.	$626^2 = 391876$ divided by $10 = 39187.6$
Stage 3: Subtract the result of stage 2 from ΣX^2_A.	$40184 - 39187.6 = 966.4$

Stage 4:

In the second bracket, square ΣX_B and divide by n_B.

$623^2 = 388129$ divided by 9 $= 43125.44$

Stage 5:

Subtract the result of stage 4 from ΣX^2_B.

$44439 - 43125.44 = 1313.56$

Stage 6:

Add the results of stages 3 and 5.

$966.4 + 1313.56 = 2279.96$

Stage 7:

Subtract 2 from the sum of n_A and n_B

$(10 + 9) - 2 = 17$

Stage 8:

Divide the result of stage 6 by the result of stage 7.

2279.96 divided by $17 = 134.115$

Stage 9:

Divide N by the product of $n_A \times n_B$.

19 divided by $10 \times 9 = 0.211$

Stage 10:

Multiply the result of stage 8 by the result of stage 9.

$134.115 \times 0.211 = 28.298$

Stage 11:

Find the square root of the result of stage 10.

$\sqrt{28.298} = 5.32$

Stage 12:

Divide the result of stage 1 by the result of stage 12.

6.6 divided by $5.32 = 1.241 = t$

Stage 13:

Find degrees of freedom $(n_A + n_B) - 2$.

$10 + 9 - 2 = 17$

Stage 14:

Consult table of critical values of t at 5 per cent ($p \leq 0.05$). For 17 df, critical value is 1.74 (one-tailed). For a two-tailed hypothesis, the critical value would have been 2.11.

Because the value of t in this case (1.241) is less than the critical value (1.74), the null hypothesis must be retained. We conclude that there is no significant difference between the times taken to sort into two and into four piles.

Pearson Product Moment correlation

The Pearson correlation coefficient is a parametric measure of correlation which reflects the linear relationship between two variables.

Rationale and assumptions

1. Because it is a parametric measure, the same assumptions apply as for a parametric test of difference (for example the two t-tests). These are:

    (a) interval or ratio level measurement;
    (b) the approximation of both samples to a normal distribution; and
    (c) homogeneity of variance (that is, both populations should have a similar spread).

2. Because it is an index of the *linear* relationship between two variables it can only be used when there is a linear (that is, straight line) relationship between the variables. That is to say that both variables must vary consistently together along all their values.

3. This limitation excludes its use where there is a curvilinear relationship betwen the two variables (see Chapter 3, Section III). Because of this limitation, you need to draw a scattergram to represent the data (see Chapter 3, Section III) to ensure the relationship is linear before proceeding.

4. The two variables must be capable of being paired in some way. This will usually be because they come from the same source.

The formula for the product moment correlation (r) is as follows:

$$r = \frac{\sum X.Y - \dfrac{(\sum X.Y)}{N}}{\sqrt{\left[\sum X^2 - \dfrac{(\sum X)^2}{N}\right]\left[\sum Y^2 - \dfrac{(\sum Y)^2}{N}\right]}}$$

where X and Y are the scores in each of the two samples and N is the number of pairs of scores.

As with the other parametric tests described earlier (the related and independent t-tests), it is a useful strategy to list the data and alongside them their squares, and in this case, their product.

Suppose Mrs Chancer had a suspicion that there was a relationship between 'highly strung children' and absenteeism from school. She measures her pupils' neuroticism using an Eysenck Junior Personality Inventory (EPI) as well as counting the number of half days each pupil had been away during the previous term. The absences scores are the X variable here, and the EPI scores are the Y variable. Because she is predicting a positive relationship between the two variables, this is a one-tailed hypothesis (that EPI and absenteeism are related).

FIGURE 4.8
Example of a Pearson's Product Moment correlation: nervous disposition (as measured by EPI) and absence from school

Absence (X)	X^2	XY	EPI (Y)	Y^2
10	100	60	6	36
12	144	96	8	64
16	256	224	14	196
7	49	63	9	81
8	64	80	10	100
10	100	70	7	49
14	196	84	6	36
20	400	240	12	144
11	121	165	15	225
$108 = \Sigma X$	$1430 = \Sigma X^2$	$1082 = \Sigma XY$	$87 = \Sigma Y$	$\Sigma Y^2 = 931$

The computation will proceed as follows:

Stage 1: Multiply ΣX by ΣY and divide by N.	$108 \times 87 = 9396$ divided by $9 = 1044$
Stage 2: Subtract the result of stage 1 from ΣXY.	$1082 - 1044 = 38$
Stage 3: In the first bracket below the line, square ΣX and divide by N.	$108^2 = 11664$ divided by $9 = 1296$
Stage 4: Subtract the result of stage 3 from ΣX^2.	$1430 - 1296 = 134$
Stage 5: In the second bracket, square ΣY and divide by N.	$87^2 = 7569$ divided by $9 = 841$
Stage 6: Subtract the result of stage 5 from ΣY^2.	$931 - 841 = 90$
Stage 7: Multiply the result of stage 4 by the result of stage 6.	$134 \times 90 = 12060$
Stage 8: Find the square root of the result of stage 7.	$\sqrt{12060} = 109.82$
Stage 9: Divide the result of stage 2 by the result of stage 8.	38 divided by $109.82 = 0.346$

Correlation coefficient $r = 0.346$. To ascertain whether this correlation is significant consult Appendix III, Table I. Critical values for a one-tailed test (degrees of freedom $N - 2$ [i.e. $9 - 2$] = 7) are 0.582 at $p \leq 0.05$ level. This is not therefore a significant correlation.

She's certainly thorough—that's only the summary.

Interpretation and Presentation of Research 5

At the end of this chapter you should be able to:

1. interpret your results in the light of the background to the research and the way the research has been designed; and
2. produce a research report which accurately reflects your work.

SECTION I   INTERPRETATION AND BACKGROUND TO RESEARCH

The results you have obtained are meaningless unless they are related to the problem currently being researched and to the previous work done in this area. An example might make this clearer. You will need to make some analysis of the way in which your results fit what others have done.

Suppose that you are looking at the Stroop phenomenon (Stroop, 1935). This suggests that when two sets of information being received by the brain are incompatible with each other, there is difficulty in dealing with them. For example, when someone is presented with words which are names of colours, in print which is a different colour from that which the colour name represents (that is, the concept which the individual has established for that label), he or she will then find it harder to deal with mentally. La Berge (1975) predicted that when printed words are presented to us, automatic reading routines are triggered which will conflict with the task of colour naming if the names of the colours are incompatible with the colour of the print. You have presented the participants in your study with two sets of words: the first, colour names printed in the colours they represent (Condition A), the second, names printed in colours incompatible with what they represent (Condition B). Participants are asked to name the colours in which the words are printed and are timed to see how long they take to do this. The findings show that participants take significantly (that is, beyond chance level) longer to respond under Condition B. You can then claim that this supports the contention of Stroop and La Berge that participants are having greater difficulty dealing with incompatible information.

This example is a fairly simple one, and the link between the time taken to respond and the difficulty of processing the information presented is straightforward, but this may not always be the case. You will, however, always need to take account in your interpretation of what has been found by others and of the theoretical proposition which underlies it – in this case that a human's brain has difficulty in dealing with incompatible information.

The hypothetico-deductive model

Scientific research is based upon the **hypothetico-deductive model**. A researcher starts with a theoretical proposition. This is then transformed into an operational or testable form by creating a hypothesis. This hypothesis carefully defines any vagueness in the theoretical proposition, replacing abstract ideas with something more concrete. In the above example, the idea of incompatibility of information becomes colour names which do not match the print colours, and 'difficulty' becomes taking longer to respond. There are limitations involved in this process of redefinition and there may be inaccuracies, but the hypothesis thus formed can be tested in a way in which the theoretical proposition cannot. This is the next stage in the process – to test the hypothesis. Then it is necessary to translate the results of this testing in terms of the theory and if necessary modify it. The newly modified theory is then translated into operational terms in a new hypothesis to be tested, and so on *ad infinitum*. Figure 5.1 represents graphically how the hypothetico-deductive model works.

What has been done by others is important at each stage. There may have been a theory formulated (for example by Stroop). Hypotheses may have been tested which may or may not embody the same definition in operational terms as that which you propose to test. Remember that theoretical propositions inevitably contain vaguenesses, which may be defined in more than one way.

FIGURE 5.1
The hypothetico-deductive model for scientific research

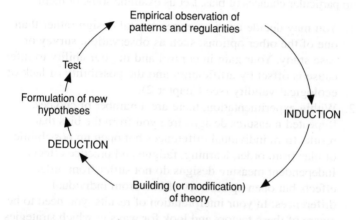

Interpretation of results and design of study

As you designed your study, you took various decisions, some of which have been highlighted in Chapter 1. It might be useful to refer back to them. They include:

- *Participants*
  You have to decide how many participants should be involved and who they should be. We have already seen that

the number of participants may affect the confidence you can have that your results are not just due to chance effects. Other factors too, such as typicality (is your sample typical of the population as a whole?), can be important. Such things as age, sex or educational and socioeconomic background may be important. Populations and samples have been discussed in Chapter 1.

● *Design of studies*

There are a number of choices available to you; these have been fully discussed in Chapters 1 and 2, Section II, and each has its implications for the interpretation of your results. When you design a study, it is a balancing act. Each decision you take opens up particular chances of bias. Let us examine some of them.

1. You may decide upon an experimental design rather than one of the other options, such as observation, survey or case study. Your gain in control and in your ability to infer cause is offset by artificiality and the possibility of lack of ecological validity (see Chapter 2).

2. Within experimentation, there are a number of choices. Repeated measures designs free you from the bias that results from individual differences but open up possibilities of bias from order, learning, fatigue and practice effects. Independent measure designs do not suffer from order effects but open up chances of bias from individual differences. In your interpretation of results, you need to be aware of these factors and look for ways in which strategies have been adopted to minimise bias – counterbalancing or randomisation for example to counter order effects, a large and representative sample to offset the effect of individual differences, together with random allocation to the conditions. Matched subject designs perhaps have the best of both these worlds, but you need to be certain that you have matched for the right characteristics.

3. Bias may also result from experimenter effects or from demand effects, as has been seen in Chapter 1. You need to be aware of this and look for strategies adopted to avoid these sources of bias – single blind or double blind studies perhaps.

4. You may have chosen a correlational design. In your interpretation of the results of your study, you need to bear in mind that you cannot infer cause from a correlational study. Also the relationship you have found may not be consistent throughout the range of values. The relationship may be a curvilinear one.

5. Choosing a survey, an observation or a case study rather than an experiment also has implications for interpretation. You have perhaps gained in ecological validity and your study is less artificial, but it is not as easy to infer cause. You have also, however, sacrificed some control, and your interpretation needs to take into account the variables which may have influenced your results.

Analysis of data and interpretation

Other factors which may have a bearing on the interpretation of the results of a study include the way in which you have analysed the data obtained. These factors include:

- the samples of the population you have tested:
- the level of measurement you are using; and
- the kind of statistical test you use and the confidence you choose.

All these things have been discussed in some detail elsewhere in this book, but it is worthwhile at this point refreshing your memory and highlighting the ways in which they may affect interpretation.

Population and samples

It is necessary to define clearly the population from which you have drawn your samples so that you are able to state clearly in your interpretation of the data how far you may legitimately generalise your findings.

Generalisability

The term **generalisability** refers to how justified you may be in applying the results of your study to people other than those whom you have actually tested. If you have defined your population carefully and taken a representative sample of that population for testing, then you can reasonably say that your results are generalisable to all the members of that population. What you cannot legitimately do is to say that because you have tested samples of a populations of boys and girls at St George's School and discovered that girls do significantly less well in Mathematics, but significantly better in English, this is true of all pupils in all secondary schools. Unless a representative sample is used of the entire population, it is not legitimate to generalise beyond the population from which you have taken a sample, although I am afraid that you will find it is frequently done! You can refer back to Chapter 1 for a fuller discussion of populations and samples.

Levels of measurement

The issue of levels of measurement relates to the amount and accuracy of the information you collect in your data. Levels of measurement are fully discussed in Chapter 3. It is sufficient at this point to say that the precision you can obtain using interval measurement is greater than that obtained with ordinal or nominal measurement. This issue of precision in measurement has two effects upon your interpretation of the data obtained:

1. There is the direct effect upon interpretation resulting from increased accuracy and precision. For example, without using any measurement at all, you might observe that girls learn to talk more quickly than boys. Using nominal measurement, you might begin to quantify this observation, taking a fixed point (say their third birthday) and a criterion for talking and counting in a representative sample, the number of boys and girls reaching that criterion. Using ordinal measurement, you might assess your sample of boys and girls for talking ability and put them in a rank order. Finally, you could use interval measurement and devise a test of talking ability yielding

talking 'scores'. As the sophistication of measurement increases, so do accuracy and precision.

2. There is an indirect effect upon interpretation which results from the use of statistical tests appropriate to the level of measurement used and the 'power' of those tests accurately to assess the probability that the result obtained was a chance one rather than the effect of the independent variable upon the dependent variable.

Confidence levels and statistical tests

Your interpretation of results will also depend upon the statistical test performed and the level of significance found. This amounts to the level of confidence you have that the results found are not due to the vagaries of chance but to the effect of the independent variable upon the dependent variable. Clearly, a 1 per cent significance level ($p \leq 0.01$) would give you great confidence in affirming that what has been found is a real psychological phenomenon, while a 5 per cent significance level ($p \leq 0.05$), although it is perfectly satisfactory, does not give you quite that confidence. If on the other hand, you have retained the null hypothesis, your results could have been due to chance alone. It is worthwhile saying at this point that if you do retain the null hypothesis and do not find significant results, you have not wasted your time. A larger sample or greater accuracy and precision in measurement might still disclose a real effect. A nonsignificant result may also be important in its own right. You are not dealing with certainties or with proof. All that you can legitimately say is that your findings support or do not support a theoretical idea.

Self-assessment questions

1. What choices have you regarding the design of your study? List some factors which might help you make your choice.
2. How far is it legitimate to generalise your results?
3. What is the relationship between the results of the research you may be carrying out and what others have done?
4. List the main elements of the hypothetico-deductive process of scientific research.

SECTION II   WRITING RESEARCH REPORTS

The final, and very important, stage in carrying out research is the writing of a report. This should be done as quickly as possible after the practical has been carried out and the data interpreted. As many researchers can testify, delaying the writing of the report only results in the whole project 'going cold'. By that is meant that your motivation may become less than it was, and essential details about why certain steps were carried out may be forgotten.

Why write a report?

There are two important reasons for writing a clear and explicit report:

1. By carefully recording and interpreting your study, you are communicating to other researchers precisely what was done and why. It should be clear, therefore, how your findings add to the store of knowledge and theory already in existence.
2. It should be possible, for those readers who wish to, to replicate your study, that is to carry it out again in exactly the way that you did. As has been noted elsewhere, replicability is a very important aspect of the scientific method. Your report is likely to be judged by whether a reader could replicate your study just from your report.

Preparing your first report

Producing an accurate and informative report is not easy, and it is worth spending a little time preparing for it before you start writing. This is particularly important when you are writing a report for the first time. There are a number of ways you can do this:

1. Look at some psychology journals, such as the *British Journal of Psychology*. Read one or two of the reports published, noting particularly their structure and the language used.
2. Read carefully any guidelines on report writing that have been provided by a tutor or which you may have received from an examining board. It is a good idea to keep these guidelines handy during the writing of your first few reports.

3. Try to get hold of some copies of past student reports. There are usually some in schools and colleges that have not been collected by previous students. Ask your tutor.

What kind of language is used?

There are a number of points to bear in mind here:

1. First, remember that much of the report will be written in the *past* tense. You are describing what has been done, how and why. This seems obvious, but it can be easy to forget in the early stages of report writing.
2. Write in simple, clear, concise sentences, using 'businesslike' language. The purpose of a report is to convey information and ideas. It is not the same as an essay, so there is no need to include long and elaborate descriptive passages. Also, it is rarely necessary to use highly technical language.
3. As far as possible, use impersonal language, for example 'The participants were shown the stimulus card' rather than 'I showed the stimulus card to the participants', or 'It seems likely that...' rather than 'I believe that...'.
4. Use nonsexist language, for example he or she rather than he, unless of course the participants are all of the same sex.
5. Do not include names of participants, and avoid anything by which they might easily be identified. Use initials, perhaps, or simply 'participant A' or 'participant B'.

How is a report structured?

There is no single correct way of structuring a report. There is, however, a generally agreed format, which tends to reflect the process of research itself. The main headings are listed below:

TITLE
ABSTRACT (SUMMARY)
INTRODUCTION
METHOD
    Design
    Participants
    Materials/apparatus
    Procedure

RESULTS
  Description
  Treatment of results
DISCUSSION
CONCLUSIONS
REFERENCES
APPENDICES

Each of these sections will be dealt with separately.

Title

This should briefly indicate the essential nature of the study and the topic under investigation. For example 'The experimental study of "Scrabble" as an aid to children's spelling' or 'A survey of gender-related attitudes towards children's play'. It is not adequate to use a title such as 'The Scrabble Experiment'.

Abstract (Summary)

This is a very brief (usually not more than 150 words) thumbnail sketch of the investigation. It should be possible for the reader to tell enough from the abstract to decide whether the report is relevant and interesting enough to read in detail.

Aim to include *(very briefly)*:

- the aim and background idea of the investigation, for example 'to investigate the effects of a memory aid on a recognition task';
- an indication of the method and/or design used, for example 'an independent measures design was used';
- a description of the participants, for example 'adult students of 'A' level';
- a description of the experimental, or other, task, for example 'participants in the experimental group were shown eight ambiguous pictures...';
- a summary of the results, for example 'a significant positive correlation was found between ratings of self-esteem and 'A' level results'; and

- a conclusion; for example 'findings appear to support Craik and Lockhart's "levels of processing" theory'.

Remember that the above points should be expressed as concisely as possible. Long abstracts are unlikely to gain full marks.

Introduction

This has two main functions:

1. It should set your study in context relative to other relevant psychological theory and research.
2. It should be structured in such a way that a hypothesis or research question emerges from your discussion of background theory and research.

A *general strategy* for this section might be as follows:

- Briefly describe the general area of research to which your study relates.
- Narrow this down to the specific theory or topic relevant to your study; it might, for example, be Craik and Lockhart's 'levels of processing' theory. This should include a brief review and a critical discussion of three or four of the relevant studies.
- Make it clear how your study is relevant to the theory and research described. This should lead naturally into a clear statement of the aims of the study.
- The aims should clearly explain what the study hopes to achieve; for example, it might be to critically assess the 'levels of processing' approach to memory by replicating one of Craik and Lockhart's studies and assessing the outcome. A full and clear statement of aims is very important. This is particularly so in more qualitative research, for example a case study, where you might not employ a specific hypothesis.
- Finally, if appropriate (always in reporting an experiment), clearly state the null and alternative hypotheses (see Chapter 1, Section I). This should be done in very precisely defined terms. For example, in an experiment to investigate the Stroop

phenomenon, 'In a card sorting task, participants will be influenced by the Stroop phenomenon' is too vague. A better hypothesis would be 'In a colour card sorting task, there will be a difference in the time taken by participants to sort cards where the ink colour conflicts with the colour name than where no conflict occurs (two-tailed)'.

Method

This section should give the reader sufficient information to be able to carry out the study in exactly the way that you have done, that is to replicate the study. It usually has four subsections, as follows:

Design

This should give a very brief indication of the general framework of the study. For example, what method was used – experiment, survey, correlational study, and so on? If it is an experiment:

- say whether it was a related or independent measures design;
- briefly describe the conditions of the experiment in relation to the independent variable: how many participants were there in each condition?; how many trials did they perform?; and
- refer to key controls used; for example, how were participants allocated to the two conditions?; was counterbalancing employed?

There is no need to give details here of how the study was carried out. This will come later in the 'Procedure' subsection.

Participants (subjects)

- Here, a brief description should be given of all participants who took part in the study. Relevant details usually include the total number, age range and sex. Other information may be relevant; for example, occupation, socioeconomic background, educational level, and so on. It is particularly important to state how participants were selected – do they form a representative sample of the population from which they are drawn, or are they an 'opportunity' sample? Particularly important too is whether or not participants were naïve, that is to say whether or not they were people with some knowledge or experience of psychological theory or of the particular theory under study.

Materials/apparatus

All materials or equipment used should be described. With questionnaires or paper and pencil tests, details of the source should be given, for example 'Concealed Shapes Test (Bloggs, 1967)', and where possible a copy placed in an appendix. Be careful to state when you have done this: for example, 'Appendix A includes a drawing of the apparatus used'. With specialist equipment, it might be helpful to include a diagram or actual examples of test materials. In some cases, a description should be included of how the materials were prepared.

Procedure

Details should be given here of precisely what was done in the investigation. Nothing should be left out. Remember it should be possible for a reader to replicate your study. This might include:

● exactly what the participants were required to do, and in what order;
● standardised instructions given to the participants;
● any controls not referred to in the 'Design' section; and
● how the performance of the participants was measured, and how the results were recorded.

Note: this should be written as a clear statement in the past tense of what was done, not as a set of instructions, such as you might have received on a lab sheet.

Results

There are two subsections here:

Descriptive statistics

Raw data should not be presented here but should be placed in an appendix and specifically referred to. This section should contain a summary of the data, usually in the form of measures of central tendency and dispersion (see Chapter 3). Bar charts, histograms or other graphical representations might also be included. Each table or chart should be clearly labelled and should have a title explaining its contents.

Treatment of results

Give details here of how the results were analysed, that is, what test of significance was used. Justify your use of the test using the guidelines in Chapter 3.

Clearly state the result of the analysis, making sure you give details of the statistic arrived at, the appropriate critical value, value of N or df, whether a one- or two-tailed test was used, whether the result is significant, and if so at what level. A typical statement might be:

The result of the related t-test was
t = 3.45, with 9 df
$p \leq 0.01$, two-tailed

State whether the null hypothesis was retained or rejected.

Note that if you wish to include calculations, these should not appear in the results section but in an appendix, specifically referred to.

Qualitative data. You may have data which are not quantitative but are nevertheless important. These may include introspections (what the participants say they feel about the study as they are taking part in it). These should be summarised and, if necessary, conclusions drawn from them. There are also perfectly valid studies where there is no quantitative measurement or statistical analysis. For example, in project 4 in Chapter 6 your data mainly consist of a transcript of a tape recording you made as you were conducting your observation. Your results will consist of a detailed analysis of this (the transcript itself will be in an appendix with excerpts in the main body of the report to illustrate the points you are making). In addition, you may have counted incidents of the techniques under study, and these can be displayed as a table. It is appropriate to comment upon your observations in a qualitative way too. It does not invalidate your work if you have no statistics or statistical test.

Discussion

This section has four main purposes:

1. To discuss and expand upon the findings presented in the results section. This should be done in such a way as to draw conclusions about the hypothesis or research question stated in the introduction.
2. To discuss the findings of your study in the light of the background literature assessed in the Introduction. To comment, also, upon any differences and similarities between your findings and those in the literature.
3. To identify the limitations of the study and modifications that might be appropriate.
4. To suggest the direction future research might take in the light of your findings.

A suggested sequence for the discussion is as follows:

- Restate the results, but in the terms of your hypothesis and without the mathematical precision and detailed analysis of the results section. For example:

   Participants did take significantly longer to sort colour cards where the ink colour conflicted with the colour name, compared with where no conflict existed.

- Comment on whether the results found were as expected and whether they confirmed the findings from other research. If not, try to suggest possible reasons for the discrepancy.
- Consider whether your findings clarify or enlarge upon a contemporary theory or extend the knowledge of a particular topic.
- Indicate whether or not the sample used allows you to generalise your findings to the population investigated. This will depend upon the extent to which the sample was

representative, bearing in mind that few samples used in psychological studies are truly representative.

- Evaluate the methods used in your study, pointing out how it could be improved in the future. Draw attention to any flaws, remembering of course not to be too 'nit-picking' about relatively minor shortcomings.
- Discuss some of the implications of your study for future research.

The main guiding principle for the discussion is to keep it *relevant*. Do not be tempted to discuss new theory or research that has not been covered in the Introduction and which is not directly relevant to your study.

Conclusions

This should be a brief re-statement of the statistical findings of the study along with a comment on the extent to which they support or refute the relevant theory or research.

References

You will need to identify the sources for both the studies you have quoted and any books and reference material you have used.

In the text, identify the main author and the date of publication, for example 'Johnson, *et al.* (1994)'.

Note: one or two authors will be referred to individually in the text, more than two as above (*et al.*).

At the end of your report, you must list all books or journal articles referred to in the body of the report.

In the References section, give full details by listing alphabetically all works you have referred to, for example:

Johnson, E, Jones T. and Shipman, S. (1994) *Psychology Review* (London: Stamford Press)

Journal articles are referenced similarly, but you will put the title of the article in full together with the journal name, volume number and page number; for example:

Zeaman D. and House B.J. (1951) The growth and decay of reactive inhibition as measured by alternation behaviour, *Journal of Experimental Psychology*, **41**, 177–201

Sometimes an article is quoted from a book of edited articles. In this case it is referenced as for the following:

Spielberger, C.D., O'Neill, H.F. and Hansen, D.N. (1972) Anxiety, drive theory and computer assisted learning, in B.A. Maher (ed.) *Progress in Experimental Personality Research* (London: Academic Press)

You should underline book titles and journal names.

Appendices

This section will contain items such as raw data, calculations, questionnaires or copies of any other items referred to in the main body of the report. Different items can be put in separate appendices – Appendix 1, Appendix 2, and so on. Refer to them in the main body of the report where appropriate.

Self-assessment questions

1. Outline some of the key decisions to be taken when designing an investigation.
2. What factors are important when interpreting the results?
3. Why is it important to write a clear and explicit report of your investigation?
4. Outline some of the characteristics of a good report.

It's no use — I can't take my mind
off my Müller-Lyer project!

Some Projects 6

The purpose of this chapter is to provide outlines of possible projects which may be used for GCE 'A' level or other coursework. It will give you the chance to put into practice some of the things which you will have read about in the previous chapters. The projects we have chosen to include are by no means prescribed though they need to be linked with the syllabus for 'A' or 'AS' level.

SECTION I   EXPERIMENTAL PROJECTS

Project 1   The Stroop phenomenon

Stroop (1935) suggested that where the format in which material is presented and the content of the information presented (for example, between the colour of the print used to print colour names and the names themselves) are incompatible, there will be greater difficulty in dealing with them than when the format and the content are compatible. La Berge (1975) suggested that our automatic reading routines are triggered when words (such as colour names) are presented, and this may interfere with the task of colour naming when there is a conflict between what is read and the information coming in from, say, the colour of the print. The aim of this experiment is to test these suggestions.

Preparation

1. Devise a hypothesis which can be tested (H_0 and H_α). In particular, define what you mean by incompatible information. Define also the form in which the colour naming will be done.
2. Decide upon the experimental design. Are you going to need to counterbalance or randomise the presentation of your material? Do you need to allocate participants randomly to the two conditions? What about other controls: standardised instructions for participants, for example?
3. Decide upon your participants.
4. Assemble materials and equipment. You will need a means of printing words in a variety of colours, some compatible with the colour names, some not. You will need a stopwatch to time the responses of your participants. There may be some difficulty in timing the very short intervals between presenting the words and the participants' response. Decide how you get over this. One way might be to present the words not one at a time, but in groups or lists, say a group of ten words. Time the responses to the whole list. Is an oral response going to be better than a written one? Are there likely to be problems standardising colour names? A list of nonsense words (of varying lengths) printed in various colours might help to test La Berge's suggestion of the automatisation of reading as well as lists where the colours and content are compatible and where they are incompatible. There is unlikely to be interference with colour naming if the words do not mean anything.
5. Decide on how results will be described and presented. What descriptive statistics will you use? What graphical representation of your results is likely to make them clearer? How will you analyse the results? What level of measurement are you using and what will be an appropriate statistical test to use?
6. Go ahead, assemble your participants, and carry out the experiment.

Project 2   Choice response time

This experiment aims to explore Hick's Law (Hick, 1952), which sets out the relationship between the number of choices available and the time taken by the brain to choose between them. It has all sorts of practical implications. For example, there are implications for motorists approaching road junctions. It is as well for road planners to keep in mind the time needed to choose between the alternative routes. Hick has suggested that the time needed to make the appropriate choice (response time, RT) will be proportional to the amount of *information* needed to decide between them. The unit of information used is the *bit* or binary unit. Where two alternatives are equally probable, one bit of information is needed to decide between them. With four possible choices two bits are needed: one to choose between two pairs of alternatives, and one to choose between the two you have initially chosen. With eight choices, you will need three bits: one to choose which four of the eight alternatives, a second to pick two of the remaining four and a third to choose between the last two. It is not unlike a Football Cup competition. Say there are 32 teams competing. The first round whittles that down to 16 (one bit). The second round (one bit) gets the number down to eight, the third round reduces the number of teams to four (one bit). The semi-finals reduce these four to two (one bit) and the finals choose between these last two (one bit). So we have five bits of information in all. This amounts to logarithms to the base 2: 32 is 2^5 ($2 \times 2 \times 2 \times 2 \times 2$), 16 is 2^4, 8 is 2^3, 4 is 2^2 and 2 is 2^1. Figure 6.1 shows logarithms to the base 2 for numbers between 1 and 99.

The way in which we suggest you set up various choices is to set participants the task of sorting playing cards. Colours (black and red) give you two choices, suits (♠ ♥ ♣ ♦) give you four choices, and numbers (excluding J, Q, K, but including A as 1) give you ten choices. You will need to measure the time taken to complete a sort of the cards.

Preparation

1. Devise hypotheses (H_0 and H_α). You will need to predict what the relationship will be between the number of choices and the

time taken. If Hick's Law holds, then participants should take 3.32 times as long to sort into ten piles (choices) as two.

FIGURE 6.1
Logarithms to base 2 for numbers between 1 and 99

n	0	1	2	3	4	5	6	7	8	9
0	–	0.00	1.00	1.59	2.00	2.23	2.59	2.81	3.00	3.17
1	3.32	3.46	3.59	3.70	3.81	3.91	4.00	4.09	4.17	4.25
2	4.32	4.39	4.46	4.52	4.59	4.64	4.70	4.76	4.81	4.86
3	4.91	4.95	5.00	5.04	5.09	5.13	5.17	5.21	5.25	5.29
4	5.32	5.36	5.39	5.43	5.46	5.49	5.52	5.55	5.58	5.61
5	5.64	5.67	5.70	5.73	5.75	5.78	5.81	5.83	5.86	5.88
6	5.91	5.93	5.95	5.98	6.00	6.02	6.04	6.07	6.09	6.11
7	6.13	6.15	6.17	6.19	6.21	6.23	6.25	6.27	6.29	6.30
8	6.32	6.34	6.36	6.38	6.39	6.41	6.43	6.44	6.46	6.48
9	6.49	6.51	6.52	6.54	6.55	6.57	6.58	6.60	6.61	6.63

---

2. Decide on your experimental design. There are clearly going to be several conditions. There is a whole range you could devise beside the three mentioned above 13, for example, for numbers including court cards. Are you going to employ a related measures design or an independent measures design? How do you intend to control for the effects of boredom, fatigue and learning/practice if you go for a related measures design? Instructions are going to be important to ensure that each sort is carried out in precisely the same way. Is it going to be possible to control the effects of different physical movements between, say, sorting into 13 piles and into two? Can you time just the movements without the mental sorting process? Then subtract these times from those which include sorting? How many sorts should be carried out under each condition?

3. Decide upon your participants, recruit them and give them their instructions. These should, of course, be standardised

and will clearly depend upon the decisions you make in 2.
4. Assemble materials and equipment. Packs of cards will need to be as similar as possible and shuffled in exactly the same way. Stopwatches will be needed to time each sort as well as some sort of pro forma on which to record your measurements.
5. Analysis of your results will clearly involve finding mean times for each condition, having first subtracted movement times. What statistical test is appropriate here? You have more than two conditions and either related or independent measures (whichever you have decided on). You are also interested in the proportionate differences in time taken. Perhaps there is a means to assess whether these proportions are significantly at odds with those which Hick proposed. Again, what kind of significance test can you employ?
6. Finally, assemble your participants and carry out your experiment.

Summary

To sum up, here is a flow chart (Figure 6.2) showing the stages in the planning of your project.

Figure 6.2
Flow chart of decisions to be taken in planning a project

Hypothesis ➤ Design ➤ Participants ➤ Materials ➤ Analysis ➤ Run

SECTION II   OBSERVATIONAL STUDIES

Project 3   Interactive techniques

Schaffer (1977) suggested that there are specific techniques which a mother employs when interacting with an infant. These are outlined in his book *Mothering*. Briefly, the techniques include the following:

- *Phasing*. This describes the way in which the mother watches for an opportunity to slot in to the child's behaviour something she wishes the child to do. Newson and Newson (1976) have illustrated this process, describing how a mother gets an infant to follow a ring dangling in front of his eyes.
- *Adaptive techniques*. This relates to the way in which a mother adapts her behaviour to that of the infant. She does not behave at all as she would if she were interacting with an adult. Movements are slower, gestures are more emphatic, expressions are exaggerated and her speech is more intermittent and simpler. There is a great deal of repetition. Stern (1977) has shown how the stimulation which a mother provides for an infant is not haphazard, but highly structured activity.
- *Facilitative techniques*. These relate to the way in which a mother makes it easier for the infant to initiate interactions. She may spend time clearing away things which are not immediately in focus, putting things next to each other so that the child will use them together or making them easier for the child to deal with, perhaps turning something round so that it is more easily grasped. Rather than overtly teaching their children, mothers spend time on what White and Watts (1973) describe as 'low keyed facilitative techniques' aimed at encouraging the child's activity, making suggestions, helping with difficulties, supplying materials, participating in what he or she is doing or lavishing praise and admiration on the efforts the child is making.
- *Elaborative techniques*. This relates to the way in which a mother first allows a child to show where his or her interest lies and then elaborates upon that interest. If a child shows interest in a toy, the mother will fetch it if it is out of reach, label it verbally, point out some of its features and demonstrate what it can do, adding a verbal dimension to the child's visual experience and allowing the child to associate sight and sound to acquire another addition to his or her vocabulary.
- *Initiating techniques*. There are times when the mother takes the initiative, but even here her behaviour is very closely linked to that of the child. Timing is important. The mother

ensures that she first catches the child's attention and then directs it to the object she wants the child to become interested in. Then she will check that the child's attention is indeed following where she is pointing.

- *Control techniques* arise out of the need for the mother to be occasionally more assertive. Even here, this is a two-way process, not the arbitrary imposition of control upon the child. There is checking to make sure that the child has understood, that it is appropriate to the child's ability to follow, there are nonverbal gestures to provide the child with help in doing what the mother wants him or her to do, and these are delivered only when the mother is sure that the child's attention is on her.

The aim of this observation is to study the extent to which these techniques which Schaffer has outlined in relation to infants and their interactions with their mothers are used by other adults in their interactions with older children. The basis will be a close observation, accompanied by a tape recording of the interactions between an adult (perhaps a father or a friend) and an older child between five and eight years old (the important thing is that the child should be old enough to be able to use language fluently) while the child is performing some manipulative task (this could be anything from baking a cake to assembling Lego or Meccano).

Preparation

1. Make a clear statement of your aims. You will need to show that the techniques noted by Schaffer will be seen also in interactions by another adult with an older child. Remember that establishing a hypothesis involves operationalising the ideas you have formulated. The kinds of behaviour you will classify under the heading of each of the techniques Schaffer lists will need to be clearly identified in relation to an older child and another adult. You will need to specify the kind of interaction you are concerned with and the time limits.
2. Design. You will be concerned with your plan of campaign. How will you ensure that the piece of behaviour you record and observe is representative? How will you make sure that both

adult and child behave in a natural way? How will you set up
the study? What instructions will be given to the participants?

3. Choose your participants. Factors to consider will include the
age of the child and the ease with which he or she is likely to
interact with the adult, how familiar the adult is with the
child, and what you propose the manipulative task should be.
Bear in mind the ethical considerations outlined in Chapter I,
Section II, for example informed consent.

4. Assemble your materials. Make sure that what the
participants will need for the task is easily available. Set up
the tape recorder and test it. Prepare yourself for observation.
Among other things you will need a checklist of points to
look for, derived from Schaffer's techniques.

5. How will you do your analysis? You have already identified
criteria by which you can judge which of the interactions you
have observed fall under which category. Replay the tape and
write a full transcript. Annotate this with your observations.
This will go into your report as raw data in an appendix.
From the transcript count incidents of each of Schaffer's
techniques. Draw up a frequency table. A bar chart will
display clearly whether your findings support the hypothesis
or not. You have only one participant so that formal
significance testing is not possible. Remember the limitations
that this will place upon the generalisability of your study.

6. Go ahead and run your observation.

Project 4   Piaget's concept of conservation

Piaget (see Birch and Malim, 1988, p 27ff) developed the idea that
children between the ages of about seven and 11 gradually
become increasingly able to conserve. This implies that they are
increasingly able to understand that while the overall appearance
of objects and materials in relation to features such as volume,
number, mass and area may change, the objects themselves remain
unchanged; their nature is 'conserved'. For example, a ball of
plasticine contains the same amount of plasticine when it is rolled
out into a sausage shape. Piaget has suggested that below the age
of about seven, children will be unable to 'conserve'. It is
suggested you could use the services of members of a primary

school or a playgroup to investigate three aspects of conservation: conservation of substance (as in the plasticine example above), conservation of volume (liquid poured from a tall beaker into a shallow bowl still retains the same volume) and conservation of number (a row of ten beads remains the same even when spread out to double its length). Later researchers have reported (in Margaret Donaldson's book *Children's Minds*; Donaldson, 1978) that children achieve conservation earlier than Piaget had suggested and that this might have been because Piaget's experiments tended to be on the adult's terms rather than the child's. When an important adult such as the experimenter spread out the beads, there must have been some real change, whereas when a 'naughty teddy' 'messed them up' this was not the case, as McGarrigle found (reported in Donaldson's book).

The aim of this observation is to test differences in 'conservation' between three to four-year-olds and children of six to seven.

Preparation

1. Approach the principal of a primary school and/or a playgroup and outline what you intend to do. Ask permission to use participants of the appropriate ages from his or her school. Obtain permission also from the parents of children participating. Take careful note of ethical considerations which need to be borne in mind (Chapter 1, section II). Establish your hypothesis. Do you predict that you will find what Piaget found or that the younger children will be able to conserve? What is your null hypothesis going to be?

2. What is the design of your observation going to be? What controls will you need to have in place? Is it going to be independent measures or repeated measures? Is it going to matter what order you test your participants in? What instructions will you give them?

3. Choose your participants. You will need a sample of children of each age. How will you ensure that it is representative, at the least, of children in that school or playgroup? You will clearly need the principal's and the class teacher's help in this.

4. Assemble the equipment you will need. Different shaped liquid containers, plasticine and beads or counters. Tables and

chairs will also be needed and perhaps a tape recorder to
record the children's responses. Again you will need to rely
upon the good offices of the principal and the class teacher.

5. How will you analyse your results ? What level of
   measurement are you going to be able to use? Is each child
   going to be marked down as conserving or not conserving, on
   each test? Is it going to be useful to include qualitative data in
   the form of some written account of how the children
   performed and introspections (how the children themselves
   said they felt about it)? How will you display your data? What
   tables, bar charts or graphs are appropriate to use? What about
   a test of significance? What level of data have you got?

6. Now go ahead and do your tests.

Project 5   A natural experiment into gender differences

There has been considerable research into the behaviour of men
and women. Birch and Malim (1988) have highlighted ways in
which the behaviour of men and women differs as a result of
socialisation. Among men, the norm is to take risks, while among
women there is a greater tendency towards caution. This may
manifest itself in the way in which people drive motor vehicles.
When they come to traffic lights at amber, men will tend to take
the risk of crossing, while women will be more likely to stop.
Similarly, after stopping at lights, men will be more likely to
move on the red and amber, while women will wait for green.

   This is in the nature of a field study. Participants will be
motorists coming to a particular set of lights where observers will
record behaviour. The aim will be to test whether risk taking in
terms of 'amber gambling' is gender specific.

Preparation

1. Establish and formulate a hypothesis, or perhaps two
   hypotheses, one concerned with stopping at the amber light,
   the other concerned with moving forward while the lights are
   still red and amber without waiting for the green. The null
   hypothesis will assume no distinction between men and
   women except for the vagaries of sampling error. The

alternative hypothesis will predict that there is a difference in the way in which men and women behave when faced with traffic lights. This is a two-tailed hypothesis.

2. Identify the design of your study. Clearly this will be an independent measures design and the measurement will be nominal (categorical). There will clearly be two categories of participant. The categories of conformity or risk taking might be more. This is a decision you will need to take. What do you classify as risk taking? 'Creeping' forward while the lights are still red, moving on the red and amber and waiting might be three. Similarly, with stopping at red, there might be more than one classification.

3. Your sample of participants will to some extent select themselves. Your decision will be to select the set of lights which you intend to observe. Should you choose an intersection or perhaps a 'pelican' crossing? Bear in mind that you need to find one where the sample is as representative as you can reasonably find. This will effect the extent to which you are going to be able to generalise.

4. If you have more than one observer it is important to establish interobserver reliability (see Chapter 2, Section V). Instructions and procedures should be carefully standardised.

5. Your equipment is likely to be minimal. It is as well to have pre-printed charts on which you can tally the participants. The conventional method of working is to tally them in fives (卌,卌,卌,II = 17). If you have set criteria involving the time after the lights have changed to amber, you might also need a stop watch (for example, you might count as amber gambling anyone crossing the lights more than two seconds after the lights change to amber). These criteria need to be clearly set beforehand.

5. This is a frequency based study so that your analysis should include a frequency table and or a bar chart. Consult Chapter 3 to ascertain what will be an appropriate test for the significance of your findings. It is an independent measures design using nominal data.

6. Go ahead and run your observation.

SECTION 111   CORRELATIONAL STUDIES

Project 6   Fin angles and the Müller-Lyer illusion

Gregory (1968) has suggested that here is a relationship between the angles of the arrowheads on the Müller-Lyer illusion and the extent of the perceived illusion. This project sets out to test his suggestion. In this classical illusion, it has been demonstrated that a line attached to outward facing arrowheads

will appear longer than an identical line attached to inward facing arrowheads.

FIGURE 6.3
An explanation of the Müller-Lyer illusion (after Gregory, 1968)

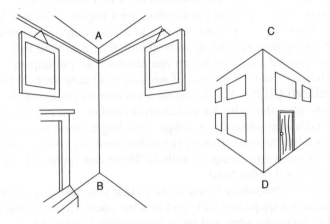

Preparation

1. The design of the study is correlational. The angles of the arrowheads in the Müller-Lyer figure will vary at 10^0

intervals between 10° and 90°, making a total of nine different arrowhead angles on both the outward facing and inward facing arrowheads. The prediction will be that there will be a relationship (that is, a positive corrrelation) between the angle of the arrowheads and the amount of the perceived illusion. This in turn supports Gregory's contention concerning the explanation for this illusion, that is, that it relates to experience of the use of constancy and distance cues. The observer is encouraged to perceive the line between outward facing arrowheads as being more distant (analogous to looking at the inside corner of a room opposite to the observer) than the line between the inward facing arowheads. Gregory draws the analogy between that and the outside corner of a building. Figure 6.3 shows what is intended. There is a fuller account of this theory in *Cognitive Processes* (Malim, 1994).

2. Each participant will be shown ten versions of the illusion with arrowheads at angles varying between 10° and 90°. The number of times each angle of arrowhead will be shown to a participant, the order in which they will be presented and the instructions given will need to be carefully considered so as to avoid **systematic error** resulting from **order or experimenter effects** (see Chapter 1). The independent variable, then, is the arrowhead angle. The important point to make in your instruction to participants is how the arrowheads should be presented, horizontally or vertically, sliding to the left or to the right. You should consider counterbalancing or randomising the way in which the arrowheads are presented. The dependent variable is the amount of illusion perceived. This may be measured in the following way.

The arrowheads are presented on a moveable slide (see Appendix II), and the participant is invited to adjust this slide until the lines between the arrowheads appear to be equal. The lines are then measured, and the difference between them is taken to be the amount of the perceived illusion. It might be important that participants are naïve, that is to say that they know nothing of the theory they are testing. In this case, you would be using a single blind study.

3. Recruit participants who are naïve, preferably nonpsychologists, as this will minimise **participant effects**. Each participant will operate independently. There might in effect be just one participant.
4. Equipment is important. The materials and method of construction are detailed in Appendix II. You will need a separate slide for each angle.
5. You will correlate two sets of data:
   (a) fin angle; and
   (b) amount of perceived illusion.
   Decide at the planning stage what technique you will adopt to obtain the correlation coefficient and how you will display your results, and the effect this might have on your choice of statistical test.
   Note: It is possible that you may end up with a curvilinear relationship. There may be a different amount of illusion perceived at extreme angles (10, 20^0 and 80, 90^0). Think about how you might display this.
6. Now go ahead and run your study.

Note: This project might equally well be run as an experiment testing whether there is a difference between the amount of illusion perceived between, say, 30^0 and 60^0 angles or horizontal and vertical presentation.

Project 7   Circadian rhythms

This study aims to examine the relationship between circadian rhythms and performance on a vigilance task. Circadian rhythms are variations throughout the 24-hour daily cycle of various physiological functions and characteristics, such as body temperature, metabolism, digestion, food intake, and so on. Horne and Osterberg, (1977), have suggested that there are 'morning types' whose performance will be best in the early part of the day and 'evening types' who are likely to perform better later in the day. There appears to be a correlation between measures of circadian activity (body temperature, for example) and performance on a vigilance task such as watching for an event which happens at infrequent intervals.

Preparation

1. You are predicting that there will be a relationship between individuals' temperature at various times of the day (or night) and a specified vigilance task. This might take the form of reaction to a visual stimulus.

2. You will need to plan the times in the day when you will test temperature as well as visual reaction time. Obviously, the more measurements you are able to make, the more conclusive your conclusions are likely to be. Each correlation will be for a particular individual but, to come to a meaningful conclusion, you will need to use several participants, to demonstrate that while there is a correlation between temperature and reaction time, the peaks and troughs will vary between individuals. Controls you will need to think about will include standardising procedures, methods of measurement and instructions to participants as well as co-researchers.

3. You will need to employ a number of participants independently of one another. The interest will be greater if they are not a homogeneous group. You need to have younger people as well as older ones, males as well as females, and individuals from different backgrounds. It might be that the differences between individuals are cultural rather than constitutional. People from a farming background, for example, become accustomed to rising early. There might be greater likelihood that they are 'morning types'.

4. You will need a thermometer. Modern instruments are very quick and easy to use. It will need to be accurate because the variations in temperature for healthy people are going to be quite small. As far as the measurement of reaction time is concerned, Piéron's technique (Piéron, 1928), reported also by Woodworth and Schlosberg (1954), is an interesting one based upon gravity. The experimenter holds a meter ruler with his or her thumb vertically against a smooth wall with its lower end against an index mark on the wall at about eye level. The participant has his or her hand poised over this mark ready to arrest its fall with his or her thumb. The experimenter says 'ready' and suddenly releases the ruler. As he or she sees the experimenter's thumb move, the participant jabs his or her own thumb down against the ruler. The

distance the ruler has fallen is then read off the ruler scale at the index mark. This can be converted into an accurate measure of reaction time using the following formula:

$$T = \frac{\sqrt{2S}}{G}$$

where T is the reaction time, S is the fall in cm and G is the acceleration due to gravity (980 cm/sec). The table below gives some falls and reaction times.

FIGURE 6.4
Reaction time in secs and fall in cm

RT	.09	.11	.12	.14	.16	.17	.18	.19	.20	.21	.22	.23	.24
F	4	6	8	10	12	14	16	18	20	22	24	26	28

A quick and easy way to deal with this is to construct a graph with the fall in cm on the base and the time in milliseconds on the vertical axis. Yet another possibility is to construct a reaction time ruler. This might prove a valuable addition to the equipment of a psychology room and is described in Appendix II.

5. Your analysis in this case will involve computing the correlation coefficient between the reaction time as measured and the time of day for a particular individual. Comparisons may be made between individuals. To avoid bias from order effects, you will need to randomise times of testing over a number of days.

6. Go ahead and run your study.

Appendices

APPENDIX I   SOME BASIC MATHEMATICAL RULES

Some symbols you may meet

X or x is used for scores (any scores)

Σ is used to indicate that what follows is to be added together

The mean is indicated by a line over a term so that $\overline{X}$ is the mean of the scores, $\overline{D}$ is the mean difference or deviation

M is sometimes also used for mean

N is used for the number of scores altogether, n for the number in one sample

D or d signifies difference or deviation

p is used for probability (of an event occuring by chance alone)

< means less than

> means greater than

$\geq$ means equal to or greater than

$\leq$ means equal to or less than

f or fr is used to indicate frequency

SD means standard deviation

χ^2 is the symbol for Chi-squared

ρ (rho) or r_s is used for a Rank Order correlation coefficient

r is used for a Product Moment correlation coefficient

√ is the symbol for square root. When a number is multiplied by itself the product is its square ($3^2 = 3 \times 3 = 9$). The reverse is the square root ($\sqrt{9}$ is 3 because $3 \times 3 = 9$). When it is placed at the beginning of a term with a line over the whole term, it implies that the square root has to be computed for the whole term once its parts have been worked out

Where an estimate has been made of a population statistic from a sample, Greek characters are employed so that:

σ (sigma) is used for an estimate of the standard deviation of a population made from a sample of it

μ (mu) is used for an estimate of a population mean from a sample of it

Computation

The order in which terms are dealt with in a formula is important:

1. Brackets ( ) or [ ] indicate that what is contained in them has to be computed first.
2. Where a symbol is placed over another, it means that the upper number has to be divided by the lower so that for example:

   $\dfrac{\Sigma}{N}$ means that the scores have to be added together and divided by the number of them

3. Then deal with division, multiplication, addition and subtraction in that order. A useful memory aid is BODMAS which stands for Brackets Over Division Multiplication Addition Subtraction.

A useful strategy to be adopted for several common computations (t-tests or Pearson's Product Moment correlation, for example) is to start by listing the scores in columns and alongside them their squares (that is, the scores multiplied by themselves) and writing down the sum of each column. Supposing that you have two samples, you can list them as follows (these are fictitious examples):

Sample A		Sample B	
X_A	X^2_A	X_B	X^2_B
12	144	14	196
16	256	23	529
19	361	10	100
23	529	10	100
17	289	18	324
25	625	12	144
12	144	30	900
16	256		

$\Sigma X_A = 140$ $\Sigma(X^2_A) = 2604$ $\Sigma X_B = 117$ $\Sigma(X^2_B) = 2293$

$[n_A = 8]$ $[n_B = 7]$

$$N = 15$$

m_A (or $\overline{X}_A$) = 17.5 m_B (or $\overline{X}_B$) = 16.7

Faced with what seems to be a very complex formula, for a t-test for independent samples, for example:

$$t = \frac{\overline{X}_A - \overline{X}_B}{\sqrt{\frac{\left\{ \Sigma X_A^2 - \frac{\left(\Sigma X_A\right)^2}{n_A} \right\} + \left\{ \Sigma X_B^2 - \frac{\left(\Sigma X_B\right)^2}{n_B} \right\}}{N-2} \times \frac{N}{n_A \cdot n_B}}}$$

you can now work like this:

Step 1   Deal with the top half of the formula first. Subtract one mean from the other, that is $17.5 - 16.7 = 0.8$.

Step 2   The lower half of the formula starts with a $\sqrt{}$ and a line covering all of it. So leave it till last. In the first bracket you have $\Sigma(X^2_A)$, which is 2604, from which you subtract $(\Sigma X_A)^2$, which is $140^2 = 19600$, divided by n_A, which is 8. This latter figure equals 2450, which when subtracted from the 2604 leaves 154.

Step 3   Treat the second bracket in the same way and you get the following: 117^2 (= 13689) divided by 7 equals 1955.57, which you subtract from 2293. This equals 337.43.

Step 4   Add the result of Step 2 to the result of Step 3 and you get 491.43.

Step 5   Divide the result of Step 4 by N – 2, which equals 15 – 2 = 13. This equals 37.8.

Step 6   Now find N (15) divided by n_A times n_B (7 × 8), that is 15 divided by 56 = 0.27.

Step 7   Multiply the result of Step 5 by the result of Step 6, 37.8 × 0.27 = 10.2.

Step 8   Find the square root of 10.2 = 3.19.

Step 9   Finally divide the result of Step 1 (the top half of the formula) by the result of Step 8 (the lower half of the formula). That is 0.8 divided by 3.19 = 0.25. This is t, and you can then consult tables to find whether your figure of 0.25 reaches the critical level for the significance level you have chosen.

Calculators

A calculator is clearly a very valuable asset in statistical computation. Ideally, you should acquire a scientific calculator with a statistical mode. Used in this mode, it is possible to enter data and obtain immediate values for the following:

n, the number of scores

$(\overline{X})$, mean

SD, standard deviation from the mean

σ, standard deviation from the mean of a population estimated from a sample of it

ΣX, the sum of the scores

ΣX^2, the sum of the squares of the scores

■ **EXERCISE A.1**

Now use the following formulae to work out the mean and standard deviation from the mean of the following data:

56
17
34
45
37
47
29
34

$$m = \frac{\Sigma x}{n} \qquad SD = \sqrt{\frac{\Sigma (M - x)^2}{n}} \qquad \sigma = \sqrt{\frac{\Sigma (M - x)^2}{n - 1}}$$

The answers are at the end of Appendix II.

APPENDIX II   DO-IT-YOURSELF PSYCHOLOGY EQUIPMENT

(adapted from *Handbook for GCE Psychology,* Brody *et al.*, 1975)

1. Müller-Lyer illusion slides

You will need:

sheets of card (two 12 × 25 cms sheets for each slide)
ruler
protractor
pencil
felt-tipped pen
Stanley knife (or similar craft knife)
gum or glue

Method

1. Rule a light pencil line along the centre of the cards.

2. 2.5 cm from the edges of the cards, draw light pencil lines parallel to it. On one card score lightly along these lines, on the other cut off the strips (see Figure A.). Fold along the scored lines.

FIGURE A
Card for Müller-Lyer apparatus

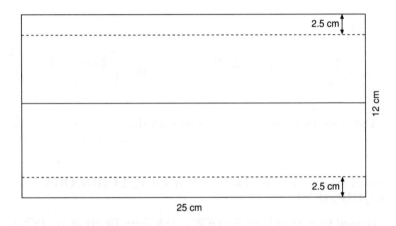

3. Glue one card to the other to form a sleeve.

4. On the outside of the sleeve, draw a line with felt-tipped pen along the centre pencil line to one edge (the right hand one is best) about 150 mm long.

5. Using a protractor, mark an angle (10, 20, 30, etc...90°: you will need a separate card for each angle) and draw a line 20 mm long on either side of the centre line to form an arrowhead. Draw another arrowhead with the same angle where the centre line meets the edge of the sleeve as in Figure B.

6. On another card mark a light pencil centre line and two parallel lines 2.9 cm on either side of the centre. Remove the two marked side strips.

FIGURE B
Sleeve with arrow

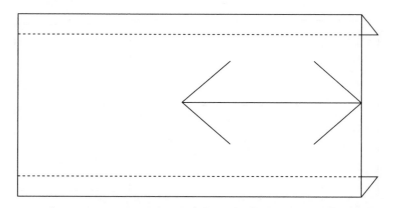

7. Rule with felt pen from the left hand edge to a point 20 mm from the right hand edge, and with a protractor mark and draw an arrowhead pointing towards the left hand edge at the same angle as on the sleeve. This forms the slide which should slide freely within the sleeve, showing a continuous centre line as in Figure C.

FIGURE C
Slide

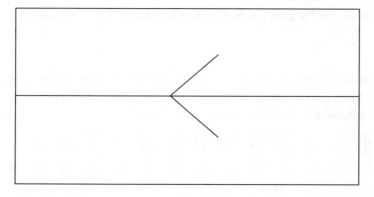

FIGURE D
Completed Müller-Lyer apparatus

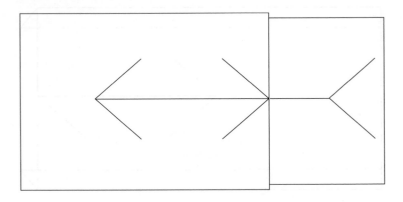

2. Reaction time ruler (see project 7)

You will need:

Strip of wood 2.5 cm × 1 meter × 6 mm thick

strip of paper to cover wood

glue

clear sticky-backed plastic

Work out for each cm of fall (S) the value of T in milliseconds.

$$T = \frac{\sqrt{2S}}{G}$$

where T is the reaction time, S is the fall in cm and G is the acceleration due to gravity (980 cm/sec). The table below gives some falls and reaction times.

RT	.09	.11	.12	.14	.16	.17	.18	.19	.20	.21	.22	.23	.24
F	4	6	8	10	12	14	16	18	20	22	24	26	28

Construct your scale marked in milliseconds. Print this on to the strip of paper and glue it on to the wood. Finally, cover in clear sticky-backed plastic to prevent deterioration. In addition to the correlation described in project 7, there are other uses for a means of measuring reaction times for instance:

- A comparison of reaction to an audible as opposed to a visual stimulus. (In this case the experimenter could blindfold participants and employ a clicker as the ruler is released.)
- A study of the latency of reaction time, that is, the effect on reaction time of the interval between the experimenter saying 'ready' and releasing the ruler. This has implications for starting races in athletics.
- A study of vigilance decrement. See *Cognitive Processes* (Malim, 1994, p 28) for a discussion of this, that is, the deterioration in reaction times to stimuli presented at infrequent intervals. Again, this has practical implications (for example, does a driver react as quickly after a long uneventful journey on a quiet road as on a busy street?).

3. Mirror drawing box

This is a valuable piece of equipment for a wide variety of experiments involving learning. You will need:

self-adhesive mirror tile 30 cm square

plywood 80 cm × 65 cm approximately

wood strengthening pieces, quarter round 12 mm

strong wood glue

Method

Cut out of the plywood the following:

1 square 30 × 30 cm to back the mirror

1 piece 30 × 32.5 cm for the base

1 piece 30 × 22.5 cm for the top

2 side pieces 32.5 × 23.75 cm with one corner removed (see Figure E).

Glue together and paint with matt black blackboard paint.

FIGURE E
Completed mirror drawing box

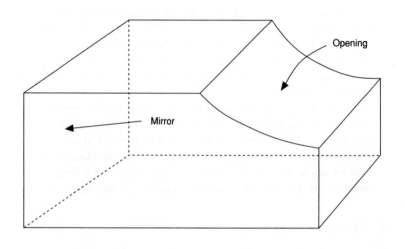

Opening

Mirror

■ ■ **ANSWERS TO EXERCISE A.1**

m = 37.375
SD = 11.987
σ = 11.213

APPENDIX III   STATISTICAL TABLES

TABLE A
A table of random numbers

01	61	16	96	94	50	78	13	69	36	37	68	53	37	31	71	26	35	03	71
46	68	05	14	82	90	78	50	05	62	77	79	13	57	44	59	60	10	39	66
00	57	25	60	59	46	72	60	18	77	55	66	12	62	11	08	99	55	64	57
24	98	65	63	21	47	21	61	88	32	27	80	30	21	60	10	92	35	36	12
28	10	99	00	27	12	73	37	99	12	49	99	57	94	82	96	88	57	17	91
07	10	63	76	35	87	03	04	79	88	08	13	13	85	51	55	34	57	72	69
92	38	70	96	92	52	06	79	79	45	82	63	18	27	44	69	66	92	19	09
99	53	93	61	28	52	70	05	48	34	56	65	05	61	86	90	92	10	70	80
93	86	52	77	65	15	33	59	05	28	22	87	26	07	47	86	96	98	29	06
18	46	23	34	27	85	13	99	24	44	49	18	09	79	49	74	16	32	23	02
24	53	63	94	09	41	10	76	47	91	44	04	95	49	66	39	60	04	59	81
22	06	34	72	52	82	21	15	65	20	33	29	94	71	11	15	91	29	12	03
07	16	39	33	66	98	56	10	56	79	77	21	30	27	12	90	49	22	23	62
29	70	83	63	51	99	74	20	52	36	87	09	41	15	09	98	60	16	03	03
57	90	12	02	07	23	47	37	17	31	54	08	01	88	63	39	41	88	92	10
33	35	72	67	47	77	34	55	45	70	08	18	27	38	90	16	95	86	70	75
49	41	31	06	70	42	38	06	45	18	64	84	73	31	65	52	53	37	97	15
65	19	69	02	83	60	75	86	90	68	24	64	19	35	51	56	61	87	39	12
92	09	84	38	76	22	00	27	69	85	29	81	94	78	70	21	94	47	90	12
98	77	87	68	07	91	51	67	62	44	40	98	05	93	78	23	32	65	41	18
00	41	86	79	79	68	47	22	00	20	35	55	31	51	51	00	83	63	22	55
57	99	99	90	37	36	63	32	08	58	37	40	13	68	97	87	64	81	07	83
12	59	52	57	02	22	07	90	47	03	28	14	11	30	79	20	69	22	40	98
31	51	10	96	46	92	06	88	07	77	56	11	50	81	69	40	23	72	51	39
96	11	83	44	80	34	68	35	48	77	33	42	40	90	60	73	96	53	97	86
85	47	04	66	08	34	72	57	59	13	82	43	80	46	15	38	26	61	70	04
72	82	32	99	90	63	95	73	76	63	89	73	44	99	05	48	67	26	43	18
91	36	74	43	53	30	82	13	54	00	78	45	63	98	35	55	03	36	67	68
77	53	84	46	47	31	91	18	95	58	24	16	74	11	53	44	10	13	85	57
37	27	47	39	19	84	83	70	07	48	53	21	40	06	71	95	06	79	88	54
44	91	13	32	97	75	31	62	66	54	84	80	32	75	77	56	08	25	70	29
37	30	28	59	85	53	56	68	53	40	01	74	39	59	73	30	19	99	85	48
75	20	80	27	77	78	91	69	16	00	08	43	18	73	68	67	69	61	34	25
65	95	79	42	94	93	62	40	89	96	43	56	47	71	66	46	76	29	67	02
05	02	03	24	17	47	97	81	56	51	92	34	86	01	82	55	51	33	12	91
94	21	78	55	09	72	76	45	16	94	29	95	81	83	83	79	88	01	97	30
34	41	92	45	71	09	23	70	70	07	12	38	92	79	43	14	85	11	47	23
53	14	36	59	25	54	47	33	70	15	59	24	48	40	35	50	03	42	99	36
88	59	53	11	52	66	25	69	07	04	48	68	64	71	06	61	65	70	22	12
65	28	04	67	53	95	79	88	37	31	50	41	06	94	76	81	83	17	16	33
73	43	07	34	48	44	26	87	93	29	77	09	61	67	84	06	69	44	77	75
48	62	11	90	60	68	12	93	64	28	46	24	79	16	76	14	60	25	51	01
28	97	85	58	99	67	22	52	76	23	24	70	36	54	54	59	28	61	71	96
02	63	45	52	38	67	63	47	54	75	83	24	78	43	20	92	63	13	47	48
76	96	59	38	72	86	57	45	71	46	44	67	76	14	55	44	88	01	62	12

77	45	85	50	51	74	13	39	35	22	30	53	36	02	95	49	34	88	73	61
29	18	94	51	23	76	51	94	84	86	79	93	96	38	63	08	58	25	58	94
72	65	71	08	86	79	57	95	13	91	97	48	72	66	48	09	71	17	24	89
89	37	20	70	01	77	31	61	95	46	26	97	05	73	51	53	33	18	72	87
81	30	15	39	14	48	38	75	93	29	06	87	37	78	48	45	56	00	84	47
83	71	46	30	49	89	17	95	88	29	02	39	56	03	46	97	74	06	56	17
70	52	85	01	50	01	84	02	78	43	10	62	98	19	41	18	83	99	47	99
25	27	99	41	28	07	41	08	34	66	19	42	74	39	91	41	96	53	78	72
63	61	62	42	29	39	68	95	10	96	09	24	23	00	62	56	12	80	73	16
68	96	83	23	56	32	84	60	15	31	44	73	67	34	77	91	15	79	74	58
87	83	07	55	07	76	58	30	83	64	87	29	25	58	84	86	50	60	00	25
49	52	83	51	14	47	56	91	29	34	05	87	31	06	95	12	45	57	09	09
80	62	80	03	42	10	80	21	38	84	90	56	35	03	09	43	12	74	49	14
86	97	37	44	22	00	95	01	31	76	17	16	29	56	63	38	78	94	49	81
85	39	52	85	13	07	28	37	07	61	11	16	36	27	03	78	86	72	04	95
97	05	31	03	61	20	26	36	31	62	68	69	86	95	44	84	95	48	46	45
75	89	11	47	11	31	56	34	19	09	79	57	92	36	59	14	93	87	81	40
09	18	94	06	19	98	40	07	17	81	22	45	44	84	11	24	62	20	42	31
84	08	31	55	58	24	33	45	77	58	80	45	67	93	82	75	70	16	08	24
79	26	88	86	30	01	31	60	10	39	53	58	47	70	93	85	81	56	39	38

TABLE B
Table of z scores and probabilities

The following table shows the proportion of the whole 'normal distribution' between the mean and a particular standard (z) score. To find the probability of that score occurring, subtract the proportion from 0.5000. For instance, the probability of a z score of 2.000 (two standard deviations from the mean) is 0.5000 − 0.4772 = 0.228.

z	\multicolumn{10}{c}{Second decimal place}

z	0	1	2	3	4	5	6	7	8	9
0.0	.0000	.0040	.0080	.0120	.0160	.0199	.0239	.0279	.0319	.0359
0.1	.0398	.0438	.0478	.0517	.0557	.0596	.0636	.0675	.0714	.0754
0.2	.0793	.0832	.0871	.0910	.0948	.0987	.1026	.1064	.1103	.1141
0.3	.1179	.1217	.1255	.1293	.1331	.1368	.1406	.1443	.1480	.1517
0.4	.1554	.1591	.1628	.1664	.1700	.1736	.1772	.1808	.1844	.1879
0.5	.1915	.1950	.1985	.2019	.2054	.2088	.2123	.2157	.2190	.2224
0.6	.2258	.2291	.2324	.2357	.2389	.2422	.2454	.2486	.2518	.2549
0.7	.2580	.2612	.2642	.2673	.2704	.2734	.2764	.2794	.2823	.2852
0.8	.2881	.2910	.2939	.2967	.2996	.3023	.3051	.3078	.3106	.3133
0.9	.3159	.3186	.3212	.3238	.3264	.3289	.3315	.3340	.3365	.3389
1.0	.3413	.3438	.3461	.3485	.3508	.3531	.3554	.3577	.3599	.3621
1.1	.3643	.3665	.3686	.3708	.3729	.3749	.3770	.3790	.3810	.3830
1.2	.3849	.3869	.3888	.3907	.3925	.3944	.3962	.3980	.3997	.4015
1.3	.4032	.4049	.4066	.4082	.4099	.4115	.4131	.4147	.4162	.4177
1.4	.4192	.4207	.4222	.4236	.4251	.4265	.4279	.4292	.4306	.4319
1.5	.4332	.4345	.4357	.4370	.4382	.4394	.4406	.4418	.4429	.4441
1.6	.4452	.4463	.4474	.4484	.4495	.4505	.4515	.4525	.4535	.4545
1.7	.4554	.4564	.4573	.4582	.4591	.4599	.4608	.4616	.4625	.4633
1.8	.4641	.4649	.4656	.4664	.4671	.4678	.4686	.4693	.4699	.4706
1.9	.4713	.4719	.4726	.4732	.4738	.4744	.4750	.4756	.4761	.4767
2.0	.4772	.4778	.4783	.4788	.4793	.4798	.4803	.4808	.4812	.4817
2.1	.4821	.4826	.4830	.4834	.4838	.4842	.4846	.4850	.4854	.4857
2.2	.4861	.4864	.4868	.4871	.4875	.4878	.4881	.4884	.4887	.4890
2.3	.4893	.4896	.4898	.4901	.4904	.4906	.4909	.4911	.4913	.4916
2.4	.4918	.4920	.4922	.4925	.4927	.4929	.4931	.4932	.4934	.4936
2.5	.4938	.4940	.4941	.4943	.4945	.4946	.4948	.4949	.4951	.4952
2.6	.4953	.4955	.4956	.4957	.4959	.4960	.4961	.4962	.4963	.4964
2.7	.4965	.4966	.4967	.4968	.4969	.4970	.4971	.4972	.4973	.4974
2.8	.4974	.4975	.4976	.4977	.4977	.4978	.4979	.4979	.4980	.4981
2.9	.4981	.4982	.4982	.4983	.4984	.4984	.4985	.4985	.4986	.4986

z	0	1	2	3	4	5	6	7	8	9
					Second decimal place					
3.0	.4987	.4987	.4987	.4988	.4988	.4989	.4989	.4989	.4990	.4990
3.1	.4990	.4991	.4991	.4991	.4992	.4992	.4992	.4992	.4993	.4993
3.2	.4993	.4993	.4994	.4994	.4994	.4994	.4994	.4995	.4995	.4995
3.3	.4995	.4995	.4995	.4996	.4996	.4996	.4996	.4996	.4996	.4997
3.4	.4997	.4997	.4997	.4997	.4997	.4997	.4997	.4997	.4997	.4998
3.5	.4998	.4998	.4998	.4998	.4998	.4998	.4998	.4998	.4998	.4998
3.6	.4998	.4998	.4999	.4999	.4999	.4999	.4999	.4999	.4999	.4999
3.7	.4999	.4999	.4999	.4999	.4999	.4999	.4999	.4999	.4999	.4999
3.8	.4999	.4999	.4999	.4999	.4999	.4999	.4999	.4999	.4999	.4999
3.9	.5000	.5000	.5000	.5000	.5000	.5000	.5000	.5000	.5000	.5000

TABLE C
Table of critical values of t

The results are significant at a particular level if the observed value of t is greater than the table value. This table gives values for a *two-tailed* test. For a *one-tailed* test, the significance levels are halved.

Degrees of freedom	Significance level, p				
	.1	.05	.02	.01	.001
1	6.31	12.71	31.82	63.657	636.62
2	2.92	4.30	6.96	9.92	31.60
3	2.35	3.18	4.54	5.84	12.92
4	2.13	2.78	3.75	4.60	8.61
5	2.01	2.57	3.36	4.03	6.87
6	1.94	2.45	3.14	3.707	5.96
7	1.89	2.36	2.99	3.499	5.41
8	1.86	2.31	2.90	3.35	5.04
9	1.83	2.26	2.82	3.25	4.78
10	1.81	2.23	2.76	3.169	4.59
11	1.80	2.20	2.72	3.106	4.44
12	1.78	2.18	2.68	3.05	4.32
13	1.77	2.16	2.65	3.01	4.22
14	1.76	2.14	2.62	2.977	4.14
15	1.75	2.13	2.60	2.947	4.07
16	1.75	2.12	2.58	2.92	4.01
17	1.74	2.11	2.57	2.898	3.96
18	1.73	2.10	2.55	2.878	3.92
19	1.73	2.09	2.54	2.86	3.88
20	1.72	2.09	2.53	2.84	3.85
21	1.72	2.08	2.52	2.83	3.82
22	1.72	2.07	2.51	2.819	3.79
23	1.71	2.07	2.50	2.807	3.77
24	1.71	2.06	2.49	2.797	3.74
25	1.71	2.06	2.48	2.787	3.72
26	1.71	2.06	2.48	2.779	3.71
27	1.70	2.05	2.47	2.77	3.69
28	1.70	2.05	2.47	2.76	3.67
29	1.70	2.04	2.46	2.756	3.66
30	1.70	2.04	2.46	2.75	3.65
40	1.68	2.02	2.42	2.70	3.55
60	1.67	2.00	2.39	2.66	3.46
120	1.66	1.98	2.36	2.617	3.37
∞	1.64	1.96	2.33	2.576	3.29

TABLE D
Table of critical values of χ^2 (Chi-squared)

The results are significant at a particular level if the observed value of χ^2 is greater than the table value. These are the values for a *two-tailed* test. For a *one-tailed* test, the significance levels are halved.

Degrees of freedom	Significance level, p			
	.05	.02	.01	.001
1	3.84	5.41	6.63	10.83
2	5.99	7.82	9.21	13.81
3	7.81	9.84	11.34	16.27
4	9.49	11.67	13.28	18.47
5	11.07	13.39	15.09	20.51
6	12.59	15.03	16.81	22.46
7	14.07	16.62	18.47	24.32
8	15.51	18.17	20.09	26.12
9	16.92	19.68	21.67	27.88
10	18.31	21.16	23.21	29.59
11	19.67	22.62	24.72	31.26
12	21.03	24.05	26.22	32.91
13	22.36	25.47	27.69	34.53
14	23.68	26.87	29.14	36.12
15	24.99	28.26	30.58	37.67
16	26.23	29.63	32.00	39.25
17	27.59	30.99	33.41	40.79
18	28.87	32.35	34.80	42.31
19	30.14	33.69	36.19	43.82
20	31.41	35.02	37.57	45.31
21	32.67	36.34	38.93	46.78
22	33.92	37.66	40.29	48.27
23	35.17	38.97	41.64	49.73
24	36.41	40.27	42.98	51.18
25	37.65	41.57	44.31	52.62
26	38.88	42.86	45.64	54.05
27	40.11	44.14	46.96	55.48
28	41.34	45.42	48.28	56.89
29	42.56	46.69	49.59	58.30
30	43.77	47.96	50.89	59.70
32	46.19	50.49	53.49	62.49
34	48.60	52.99	56.06	65.25
36	50.99	55.49	58.62	67.98
38	53.38	57.97	61.16	70.70
40	55.76	60.44	63.69	73.40
42	58.12	62.89	66.21	76.08
44	60.48	65.34	68.71	78.75
46	62.83	67.77	71.20	81.40
48	65.17	70.12	73.68	84.04
50	67.50	72.61	76.15	86.66

TABLE E
Table of critical values of X for the Sign test

Results are significant if the observed value of X is equal to or less than the table value. N represents the total number of signs. Note that any zeros are not included in N. This table gives values for a *two-tailed* test. For a *one-tailed* test, the significance levels are halved.

	Significance level, p						**Significance level, p**			
N	**0.1**	**0.05**	**0.02**	**0.01**		**T**	**0.1**	**0.05**	**0.02**	**0.01**
5	0					30	10	9	8	7
6	0	0				31	10	9	8	7
7	0	0	0			32	10	9	8	8
8	1	0	0	0		33	11	10	9	8
9	1	1	0	0		34	11	10	9	9
10	1	1	0	0		35	12	11	10	9
11	2	1	1	0		36	12	11	10	9
12	2	2	1	1		37	13	12	10	10
13	3	2	1	1		38	13	12	11	10
14	3	2	2	1		39	13	12	11	11
15	3	3	2	2		40	14	13	12	11
16	4	3	2	2		41	14	13	12	11
17	4	4	3	2		42	15	14	13	12
18	5	4	3	3		43	15	14	13	12
19	5	4	4	3		44	16	15	13	13
20	5	5	4	3		45	16	15	14	13
21	6	5	4	4		46	16	15	14	13
22	6	5	5	4		47	17	16	15	14
23	7	6	5	4		48	17	16	15	14
24	7	6	5	5		49	18	17	15	15
25	7	7	6	5						
26	8	7	6	6						
27	8	7	7	6						
28	9	8	7	6						
29	9	8	7	7						

TABLE F
Table of critical values of T for the Wilcoxon test

Results are significant at a particular level if the observed value of T is smaller than the table value. This table gives values for a *two-tailed* test. For a *one-tailed* test, the significance levels are halved.

	Significance level, p			
N	0.100	0.050	0.020	0.010
5	0			
6	2	0		
7	3	2	0	
8	5	3	1	0
9	8	5	3	1
10	10	8	5	3
11	13	10	7	5
12	17	13	9	7
13	21	17	12	9
14	25	21	15	12
15	30	25	19	15
16	35	29	23	19
17	41	34	27	23
18	47	40	32	27
19	53	46	37	32
20	60	52	43	37
21	67	58	49	42
22	75	65	55	48
23	83	73	62	54
24	91	81	69	61
25	100	89	76	68
26	110	98	84	75
27	119	107	92	83
28	130	116	101	91
29	140	126	110	100
30	151	137	120	109

TABLE G
Table of critical values of U or U_1 for the Mann-Whitney test

For each value of N_S and N_L there are two numbers. The top one is the value of U which **must not be exceeded** for significance at the 0.005 level for a *one-tailed* test (0.01 for a *two-tailed* test); the lower one gives the value for the 0.025 level for a *one-tailed* test (0.05 for a *two-tailed* test).

N_S	1	2	3	4	5	6	7	8	9	10	11	12	13	14	15	16	17	18	19	20
N_L																				
2	–	–	–	–	–	–	–	–	–	–	–	–	–	–	–	–	–	–	0	0
	–	–	–	–	–	–	–	0	0	0	0	1	1	1	1	1	2	2	2	2
3	–	–	–	–	–	–	–	–	0	0	0	1	1	1	2	2	2	2	3	3
	–	–	–	–	0	1	1	2	2	3	3	4	4	5	5	6	6	7	7	8
4	–	–	–	–	–	0	0	1	1	2	2	3	3	4	5	5	6	6	7	8
	–	–	–	0	1	2	3	4	4	5	6	7	8	9	10	11	11	12	13	14
5	–	–	–	–	0	1	1	2	3	4	5	6	7	7	8	9	10	11	12	13
	–	–	0	1	2	3	5	6	7	8	9	11	12	13	14	15	17	18	19	20
6	–	–	–	0	1	2	3	4	5	6	7	8	10	11	12	13	15	16	17	18
	–	–	1	2	3	5	6	8	10	11	13	14	16	17	19	21	22	24	25	27
7	–	–	–	0	1	3	4	6	7	9	10	12	13	15	16	18	19	21	22	24
	–	–	1	3	5	6	8	10	12	14	16	18	20	22	24	26	28	30	32	34
8	–	–	–	1	2	4	6	7	9	11	13	15	17	18	20	22	24	26	28	30
	–	0	2	4	6	8	10	13	15	17	19	22	24	26	29	31	34	36	38	41
9	–	–	0	1	3	5	7	9	11	13	16	18	20	22	24	27	29	31	33	36
	–	0	2	4	7	10	12	15	17	20	23	26	28	31	34	37	39	42	45	48
10	–	–	0	2	4	6	9	11	13	16	18	21	24	26	29	31	34	37	39	42
	–	0	3	5	8	11	14	17	20	23	26	29	33	36	39	42	45	48	52	55
11	–	–	0	2	5	7	10	13	16	18	21	24	27	30	33	36	39	42	45	48
	–	0	3	6	9	13	16	19	23	26	30	33	37	40	44	47	51	55	58	62
12	–	–	1	3	6	9	12	15	18	21	24	27	31	34	37	41	44	47	51	54
	–	1	4	7	11	14	18	22	26	29	33	37	41	45	49	53	57	61	65	69
13	–	–	1	3	7	10	13	17	20	24	27	31	34	38	42	45	49	53	57	60
	–	1	4	8	12	16	20	24	28	33	37	41	45	50	54	59	63	67	72	76
14	–	–	1	4	7	11	15	18	22	26	30	34	38	42	46	50	54	58	63	67
	–	1	5	9	13	17	22	26	31	36	40	45	50	55	59	64	69	74	78	83
15	–	–	2	5	8	12	16	20	24	29	33	37	42	46	51	55	60	64	69	73
	–	1	5	10	14	19	24	29	34	39	44	49	54	59	64	70	75	80	85	90
16	–	–	2	5	9	13	18	22	27	31	36	41	45	50	55	60	65	70	74	79
	–	1	6	11	15	21	26	31	37	42	47	53	59	64	70	75	81	86	92	98
17	–	–	2	6	10	15	19	24	29	34	39	44	49	54	60	65	70	75	81	86
	–	2	6	11	17	22	28	34	39	45	51	57	63	69	75	81	87	93	99	105
18	–	–	2	6	11	16	21	26	31	37	42	47	53	58	64	70	75	81	87	92
	–	2	7	12	18	24	30	36	42	48	55	61	67	74	80	86	93	99	106	112
19	–	0	3	7	12	17	22	28	33	39	45	51	57	63	69	74	81	87	93	99
	–	2	7	13	19	25	32	38	45	52	58	65	72	78	85	92	99	106	113	119
20	–	0	3	8	13	18	24	30	36	42	48	54	60	67	73	79	86	92	99	105
	–	2	8	14	20	27	34	41	48	55	62	69	76	83	90	98	105	112	119	127

TABLE H
Table of critical values of r_s (ρ) for the Spearman's Rank Order correlation.

N is the number of paired scores. r_s (ρ) must be equal to or greater than the table value to be significant.

	Level of significance for one-tailed test			
	0.05	0.025	0.01	0.005
	Level of significance for a two-tailed test			
N	0.01	0.05	0.02	0.01
5	0.900	1.000	1.000	–
6	0.829	0.886	0.943	1.000
7	0.714	0.786	0.893	0.929
8	0.643	0.738	0.833	0.881
9	0.600	0.683	0.783	0.833
10	0.564	0.648	0.746	0.794
12	0.506	0.591	0.712	0.777
14	0.456	0.544	0.645	0.715
16	0.425	0.506	0.601	0.665
18	0.399	0.475	0.564	0.625
20	0.377	0.450	0.534	0.591
22	0.359	0.428	0.508	0.562
24	0.343	0.409	0.485	0.537
26	0.329	0.392	0.465	0.515
28	0.317	0.377	0.448	0.496
30	0.306	0.364	0.432	0.478

TABLE I
Table of critical values of r for the Pearson Product Moment correlation

Results are significant at a particular level if the correlation r is equal to or greater than the table value. N is the number of pairs of scores.

	Level of significance for one-tailed test			
	0.05	0.025	0.005	0.0005
	Level of significance for a two-tailed test			
N – 2	0.10	0.05	0.01	0.001
2	0.9000	0.9500	0.9900	0.9999
3	0.805	0.878	0.9587	0.9911
4	0.729	0.811	0.9172	0.9741
5	0.669	0.754	0.875	0.9509
6	0.621	0.707	0.834	0.9241
7	0.582	0.666	0.798	0.898
8	0.549	0.632	0.765	0.872
9	0.521	0.602	0.735	0.847
10	0.497	0.576	0.708	0.823
11	0.476	0.553	0.684	0.801
12	0.457	0.532	0.661	0.780
13	0.441	0.514	0.641	0.760
14	0.426	0.497	0.623	0.742
15	0.412	0.482	0.606	0.725
16	0.400	0.468	0.590	0.708
17	0.389	0.456	0.575	0.693
18	0.378	0.444	0.561	0.679
19	0.369	0.433	0.549	0.665
20	0.360	0.423	0.537	0.652
25	0.323	0.381	0.487	0.597
30	0.296	0.349	0.449	0.554
35	0.275	0.325	0.418	0.519
40	0.257	0.304	0.393	0.490
45	0.243	0.288	0.372	0.465
50	0.231	0.273	0.354	0.443
60	0.211	0.250	0.325	0.408
70	0.195	0.232	0.302	0.380
80	0.183	0.217	0.283	0.357
90	0.173	0.205	0.267	0.338
100	0.164	0.195	0.254	0.321

TABLE J
Table of critical values of F

Results are significant at the 5 per cent level if the observed value of F is greater than the table value. To test homogeneity of variance, divide the variance of one population by that of the other. The result is F. There is homogeneity of variance if F is not significant.

		df_L						
		1	**2**	**3**	**4**	**5**	**6**	**7**
	1	648	800	864	900	922	937	948
	2	38.50	39.00	39.17	39.24	39.30	39.33	39.35
	3	17.44	16.04	15.44	15.10	14.89	14.74	14.62
	4	12.22	10.65	9.98	9.60	9.36	9.20	9.07
	5	10.01	8.43	7.76	7.39	7.15	6.98	6.85
	6	8.81	7.26	6.60	6.23	5.99	5.82	5.70
	7	8.07	6.54	5.89	5.52	5.29	5.12	4.99
	8	7.57	6.06	5.42	5.05	4.82	4.66	4.53
	9	7.21	5.71	5.08	4.72	4.48	4.32	4.20
	10	6.94	5.46	4.83	4.47	4.24	4.07	3.95
	11	6.72	5.26	4.63	4.28	4.04	3.88	3.76
df_s	12	6.55	5.10	4.47	4.12	3.89	3.73	3.61
	13	6.41	4.97	4.35	4.00	3.77	3.60	3.48
	14	6.30	4.86	4.24	3.89	3.66	3.50	3.38
	15	6.20	4.76	4.15	3.80	3.58	3.41	3.29
	16	6.12	4.69	4.08	3.73	3.50	3.34	3.22
	17	6.04	4.62	4.01	3.66	3.44	3.28	3.16
	18	5.98	4.56	3.95	3.61	3.38	3.22	3.10
	19	5.92	4.51	3.90	3.56	3.33	3.17	3.05
	20	5.87	4.46	3.86	3.51	3.29	3.13	3.01
	21	5.83	4.42	3.82	3.48	3.25	3.09	2.97
	22	5.79	4.38	3.78	3.44	3.22	3.05	2.93
	23	5.75	4.35	3.75	3.40	3.18	3.02	2.90
	24	5.72	4.32	3.72	3.38	3.15	2.99	2.87

		8	9	10	12	15	20	24
					df_1			
	1	957	963	969	977	985	993	997
	2	39.37	39.39	39.40	39.42	39.43	39.45	39.4
	3	14.54	14.47	14.42	14.34	14.25	14.17	14.1
	4	8.98	8.90	8.84	8.75	8.66	8.56	8.51
	5	6.76	6.68	6.62	6.52	6.43	6.33	6.28
	6	5.60	5.52	5.46	5.37	5.27	5.17	5.12
	7	4.90	4.82	4.76	4.67	4.57	4.47	4.42
	8	4.43	4.36	4.30	4.20	4.10	4.99	3.95
	9	4.10	4.03	3.96	3.87	3.77	3.67	3.61
	10	3.85	3.78	3.72	3.62	3.52	3.42	3.37
	11	3.66	3.59	3.52	3.43	3.33	3.23	3.17
df_s	12	3.51	3.44	3.37	3.28	3.18	3.07	3.02
	13	3.39	3.31	3.25	3.15	3.05	2.95	2.89
	14	3.29	3.21	3.15	3.05	2.95	2.84	2.79
	15	3.20	3.12	3.06	2.96	2.86	2.76	2.70
	16	3.12	3.05	2.99	2.89	2.79	2.68	2.63
	17	3.06	2.99	2.92	2.82	2.72	2.62	2.56
	18	3.01	2.93	2.87	2.77	2.67	2.58	2.50
	19	2.96	2.81	2.82	2.72	2.62	2.53	2.45
	20	2.91	2.84	2.77	2.68	2.57	2.46	2.41
	21	2.87	2.80	2.73	2.64	2.53	2.42	2.37
	22	2.84	2.76	2.70	2.61	2.50	2.39	2.33
	23	2.81	2.73	2.67	2.57	2.47	2.36	2.30
	24	2.78	2.70	2.64	2.54	2.44	2.33	2.27

Bibliography

Ainsworth, M.D.S. and Bell, S.M. (1969) Some contemporary patterns of mother infant interaction in the feeding situation, in A. Ambrose (ed.) *Stimulation in Early Infancy* (London: Academic Press)

Asch, S.E. (1952) *Social Psychology* (Englewood Cliffs: Prentice Hall)

Birch, A. and Malim, T. (1988) *Developmental Psychology: from Infancy to Adulthood* (Basingstoke: Macmillan)

British Psychological Society (1990) *Ethical Principles for Conducting Research with Human Participants*, Leicester, The British Psychological Society

Claxton, G. (1980) Cognitive Psychology: a suitable case for treatment?, in G. Claxton (ed.) *Cognitive Psychology: New Directions* (London: Routledge & Kegan Paul)

Clegg, F. (1982) *Simple Statistics* (Cambridge: Cambridge University Press)

Craik, F. and Lockhart, R. (1972) Levels of processing, *Journal of Learning and Verbal Behaviour*, **11**, 671–84

Davies, G. (1992) Teaching ethical issues: some examples from research with human participants, *Psychology Teaching New Series*, No 1, 11–19

Davies, G., Haworth, G. and Hirschler, S. (1992) Ethics in psychological research: guide-lines for students at pre-degree levels, *Psychology Teaching New Series*, No. 1, 4–10

Donaldson, M. (1978) *Children's Minds* (London: Fontana)

Eysenck, H.J. and Eysenck, S.B.G. (1964) *Manual of the Eysenck Personality Inventory* (London: University of London Press)

Gregory, R.L. (1968) Visual illusions, in *Psychology in Progress: Readings from Scientific American* (San Francisco: Freeman)

Hargreaves, D.H. (1967) *Social Relations in a Secondary School* (London: Routledge & Kegan Paul)

Harré, R. (1979) *Social Being* (Oxford: Basil Blackwell)

Hartmann, E.L. (1973) *The Functions of Sleep* (Newhaven Ct.: Yale University Press)

Heather, N. (1976) *Radical Perspectives in Psychology* (London: Methuen)

Hess, E.H. (1959) Imprinting, *Science,* **130**, 133–41

Hick, W.F. (1952) On the rate of gain of information, *Quarterly Journal of Experimental Psychology*, **4**, 11

Hill, C.J., Rubin, Z. and Peplau, L.A. (1976) Break ups before marriage: the end of 103 affairs, *Journal of Social Issues,* **32**(1), 147–88

Horne, J.A. and Osterberg, O. (1977) Individual differences in human circadian rhythms, *Biological Psychology*, **5**, 179–90

Humphrey, G. (ed.) (1963) *Psychology through Experiment* (London: Methuen)

Kadushin, A. (1976) Adopting older children: a summary of its implications, in A.M. Clarke and A.D.B. Clarke (eds) *Early Experience: Myth and Evidence* (London: Open Books)

La Berge, D. (1975) Acquisition of automatic processing in perceptual and associative learning, in P.M.A. Rabbitt and S. Dormic (eds) *Attention and Performance vol.5*, (London: Academic Press)

Luce, G.G. (1971) *Body Time: Physiological Rhythms and Social Stress* (New York: Pantheon)

Lynch, K. (1960) *The Image of the City* (Cambridge Mass.: MIT Press)

Malim, T. (1994) *Cognitive Processes* (Basingstoke: Macmillan)

Malim, T., Birch, A. and Wadeley, A. (1992) *Perspectives in Psychology* (Basingstoke, Macmillan)

Malinowski, B. (1927) *Sex and Repression in Savage Society* (New York: Harcourt Brace Jovanovich)

Marsh, P., Rosser, E. and Harré, R. (1978) *Rules of Disorder* (London: Routledge)

Massarik, F. (1981) The interviewing process re-examined, in P. Reason and J. Rowan (eds) *Human Enquiry: A Source Book of New Paradigm Research* (Chichester: John Wiley)

Masters, W.H. and Johnson, V.E. (1966) *Human Sexual Response* (Boston, Mass.: Little Brown)

Monk, T.H., Weitzman, E.D, Fookson, J.E., Moline, M.L., Kronauer, R.E. and Gander, P.H. (1983) Task variables determine which biological clock controls circadian rhythms in human performance, *Nature,* **304**, 543–5

Morris, J.B. and Beck, A.T. (1974) The efficacy of anti-depressant drugs: a review of the research (1958–72), *Archives of General Psychiatry,* **30**, 667–78

Namikas, J. and Wehmer, F. (1978) Gender composition of litter affected the behaviour of male mice, *Behavioural Biology,* **23**, 219–24

Neisser, U. (1982) *Memory Observed: Remembering in Natural Contexts* (San Francisco: W.H. Freeman)

Newson, J. and Newson, E. (1976) On the social origins of symbolic functioning, in V.P. Varma and P. Williams (eds) *Rager, Psychology and Education* (London: Hodder and Stoughton)

Ora, J.P. (1965) Characteristics of the volunteer for psychological investigation, *Office of Naval Research Contract 2149 (03)*, Technical Report 27

Orne, M.T. (1962) On the social psychology of the psychological experiment: with particular reference to demand characteristics and their implications, *American Psychologist,* **17**, 776–83

Orne, M.T. and Evans, F.J. (1965) Social control in the psychological experiment: antisocial behaviour and hypnosis, *Journal of Personality and Social Psychology,* **51**, 189–200

Ostberg, O. (1973) Circadian rhythms of food intake and oral temperature in 'morning' and 'evening' groups of individuals. *Ergonomics,* **16**, 203–9

Peterson, L.R and Peterson, M. (1959) Short term retention of individual verbal items, *Journal of Experimental Psychology*, **58**, 193–8

Piéron, H. (1928) Technique de laboratoire et appareils, *American Psychologist*, **27**, 234ff

Popper, K. (1972) *Conjectures and Refutations: the Growth of Scientific Knowledge*, 4th edn (London: Routledge & Kegan Paul)

Rogers, C.R. (1961) *On Becoming a Person: A Therapist's View of Psychotherapy* (Boston, Mass.: Houghton Mifflin)

Rosenthal, R. (1966) *Experimenter Effects in Behavioral Research* (New York: Appleton Century Crofts)

Rushton, J.P. (1978) Urban density and altruism, helping strangers in a Canadian city, suburb and small town, *Psychological Reports*, **33**, 987–90

Rutter, M., Maughan, B., Mortimore, P. and Ouston, J. (1979) *Fifteen Thousand Hours* (London: Open Books)

Schaffer, H.R. (1977) *Mothering* (London: Fontana)

Sears, D.O. (1986) College sophomores in the laboratory: influences of a narrow data base on social psychology's views of human nature, *Journal of Personality and Social Psychology*, **15**, 515–30

Stephenson, W.U. (1953) *The Study of Behaviour* (Chicago: University of Chicago Press)

Stern, D.N. (1977) The infant's stimulus world during social interaction, in H.R. Schaffer (ed.) *Studies in Mother–Infant Interaction* (London: Fontana)

Stroop, J.R (1935) Studies of interference in serial verbal reactions, *Journal of Experimental Psychology*, **18**, 643–62

Sylva, K.D., Roy C. and Painter M. (1980) *Childwatching at Playgroup and Nursery School* (London: Grant McIntyre)

Tedeschi, J.T., Lindskold, S. and Rosenfeld, P. (1985) *Introduction to Social Psychology* (New York: West)

Tinbergen, N. and Perdeck, E.C. (1950) On the stimulus situation releasing the begging response in the newly hatched herring gull chick, *Behaviour*, **3**, 1–39

Weber, S.J and Cook, T.D. (1972) Subject effects in laboratory research: an examination of subject roles, demand characteristics and valid inference, *Psychological Bulletin*, **77**, 273–95

White, B.L. and Watts, J.C. (1973) *Experience and Environment* (New York: Prentice Hall)

Whyte, W.F. (1955) *Street Corner Society: the social structure of an Italian slum* (Chicago: Chicago University Press)

Witkin, H.R., Goodenough, D.R., Karp, S.A. Dyke, R.B. and Faterson, H.F. (1962) *Psychological Differentiation* (New York: John Wiley)

Woodworth, R.S. and Schlosberg, H. (1954) *Experimental Psychology* (London: Methuen)

Index